Wildflowers of Pennsylvania

By

Mary Joy Haywood, RSM, Ph. D. and Phyllis Testal Monk, M. Ed.

and

Members of the Botanical Society of Western Pennsylvania

ISBN: 0-9710614-0-8

Published by Venture Graphics Inc. in association with
Pixel Digital Resources and ComDoc.

CONTENTS

Dedicated to all living and deceased members of the Botanical Society of Western Pennsylvania who generously and graciously shared their knowledge of plants and habitats throughout the one hundred and seven years of the Society's existence.

Scenes of
Pennsylvania

Photos by Phyllis Monk

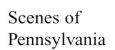

Forward

This book is intended for all who enjoy nature and would like to become more acquainted with wildflowers. Since the advent of suburban living there is much less contact with nature, and inner city living has made many people strangers to the magnificent display of plants that people took for granted in the early part of the 20th century. Yet there are many areas that are relatively untouched by modern expansion, and a visit to these areas can be a refreshing experience. A hike in the woods can restore one's feeling of being part of nature. Just as we like to know a person's name, knowing the names of plants gives one a kinship with them.

The purpose of this book is to help the observer to identify the plants seen on a spring, summer, or fall hike in a natural area. We have chosen to use photographs of the plants since they reveal much more detail than can be found in drawings. Also, the pictures are often quite beautiful. We have chosen to illustrate mostly herbaceous species that grow in Pennsylvania, omitting most flowering shrubs and trees. Many of these plants grow throughout the northeastern quarter of the United States, so the book will be useful to residents and visitors of surrounding states. For the person who wants further information about the plants in this book we have included a bibliography that will provide more technical information, and other approaches to help identify plants.

The book is organized according to the most recent taxonomy of plant families accepted by many professional botanists. This will show relationships between members of the same plant family. After the scientific name the reader will find an abbreviation of the "author" of that name. This individual has made a study of that plant and proposed the name and where the plant should be placed in relation to other species. Although the use of technical terms in the descriptions of the plants has been limited, two glossaries are included. Simple line drawings of leaf forms and flowering types may be found on the inside covers. In the descriptions the term "Introduced" is used to identify a non-native species that may have been deliberately brought from another area, or has come to Pennsylvania from another area accidentally. Often these plants have established themselves to the detriment of native species.

The authors would like to acknowledge the following; Rosemary Flaherty, RSM, for editing assistance, the photographer-members of the Society who provided the photographs, and the generosity of Carlow College for providing the facility for our meetings.

This publication is supported in part by grants from the Sisters of Mercy of the County of Allegheny, Mary Jane Longo, the Snee-Rinehardt Charitable Foundation, and the Laurel Foundation.

Phyllis Testal Monk, M. Ed.

Introduction

The invitation read, "You are requested to attend a CONFERENCE OF BOTANISTS at 35 Federal Street, Allegheny City, Thursday evening, October 7th at 7-12 o'clock." The matter of forming a Botanical Society was then fully discussed and with a motion of Mr. J.D. Shafer the name of "The Botanical Society of Western Pennsylvania" was adopted.

The Botanical Society of Western Pennsylvania has for its stated object: "to bring together those who are interested in Botany and to encourage the study of this science and a knowledge of plants."

The Botanical Society also records a list of members, summaries of presentations, summaries of field trips, and the plants located in certain areas, primarily of Pennsylvania.

Field trips were begun early after the founding of the Society. These trips included, trips in 1886 to Wildwood; 1892, Allegheny Valley Railroad Station; 1893, Login's Ferry [sic], and 1895 to the Saltworks Station on the Baltimore and Ohio Railroad. With precedence established, the Botanical Society of today, continues weekly field trips from early spring to late fall and maintains records of the plants observed. Many members venture far and wide and return to enrich us with their new findings, usually presenting them at our monthly meetings.

From its founding, the city of Pittsburgh has always been blessed with an abundance of professional individuals. The Academy of Science and Art, founded in 1890, served as a repository for independent organizations of science and art in the area. Nine Societies existed under the umbrella of the Academy of Science and Art, the Botanical Society of Western Pennsylvania being one of them. In 1881, Andrew Carnegie offered to build a library for the City of Pittsburgh. This offer was rejected due to certain legal obstacles at that time. Instead, the Academy secured the "Thaw Homestead," which was located at the southwest corner of Fifth (now Stanwix) Street and Duquesne Way in downtown Pittsburgh. Andrew Carnegie, being impressed by the events of the Academy, made an acceptable offer to build the Carnegie Library and Music Hall. A museum and rooms for accommodating the various learned Societies was included in his proposal leading to the formal opening of the Carnegie Museum in 1895.

As the Museum was anxious to build up as large a collection of mounted specimens of plants as possible, the Botanical Society of Western Pennsylvania transferred its 20,000 mounted specimens to the herbarium on November 9, 1899, with the stipulation that the members of the Society have access and use of the herbarium. The Society has since then, added thousands of additional voucher specimens to the herbarium collection. Excellent slide collections have also been donated to the Section of Botany of the Carnegie Museum of Natural History by members of the Society.

Rapid expansion of educational facilities arose: Western University of Pittsburgh now the University of Pittsburgh, moved from the North Side in 1911, followed by the founding of the Carnegie Institute of Technology, now Carnegie

Mellon University. As can be seen, the Botanical Society of Western Pennsylvania, founded in 1886, actually predates the above educational institutions.

On the centennial of our founding, October 7, 1986, the idea of publishing a book on THE WILDFLOWERS OF PENNSYLVANIA was brought forth and endorsed by the members of the Society. At that time, there was not a field guide depicting some of the common, and occasionally, the not-so-common wildflowers of Pennsylvania. An important concern of the members of the Society was to publish a field guide at a cost that would make the book available to all, especially families and amateur botanists who wished to "walk our woods and fields" and be able to identify the beautiful plants encountered therein. By enjoying these nature walks, hopefully, the reader will also recognize the necessity of habitat protection, which is essential for plant preservation. Many of our plants are in great jeopardy due to excessive construction of strip malls, strip and long-wall mining, and pollution of, not only our open spaces, but of our beautiful streams and rivers with which we as a State are so blessed. Habitat protection of very rare and endangered species of plants, led our Society to join with the Audubon Society of Erie and purchase the Titus Bog, thus saving the bog habitat from certain destruction as well as the plants growing in it.

This book is not intended as a scientific treatise. The process for this publication was initiated by asking the members to submit a list of plants to be incorporated into the work. A book committee was formed and selection of plants to be included was determined. It was concluded that almost every plant selected would have an accompanying photograph from a slide taken by members of the Society.

The Botanical Society of Western Pennsylvania, takes great pride in the fact that this Society has been active since its founding. Today, the Members are frequently called upon to lend their expertise to many undertakings, primarily in Pennsylvania.

In 1985, we were called upon to do a Survey of the Great Meadow and Battlefield of Fort Necessity. This undertaking was sponsored in part by a grant from the Department of Environmental Resources, with a matching grant from the United States Department of the Interior. In 1987, another grant was received from the DEP to do a Checklist of the Flora at the National Historic Site of Friendship Hill. An additional study supported in part by the Pittsburgh History and Landmarks Foundation was to make a checklist of the Flora of Schenley Park. Many members have been called upon to survey and record plants in specific areas attesting to the knowledge possessed by the members of this Society.

Mary Joy Haywood, RSM, Ph.D.
President, Botanical Society of Western Pennsylvania
Pittsburgh, PA, in the year 2000

Magnoliopsida
Dicots

The seeds of these flowering plants have two cotyledons. Flower parts are usually in fours and fives. The leaf veins are minutely branched forming a network. The vascular tissue is grouped in discrete bundles that form a ring underneath the outer covering of the stem. In addition to the primary vascular tissue there is secondary vascular tissue which has cells adapted for strength and support contributing to the woody nature of some of this group. Some woody examples include the Mountain Laurel and Rhododendron; herbaceous examples are the Violet, Jewelweed, and Dandelion. There are over 1250 species in Pennsylvania making this one of the richest areas in the United States in plant diversity.

Long-spurred Violet   Mary Joy Haywood

SAURURACEAE
Lizard's Tail Family

The plants of this family have 3 to 8-foot succulent stems. A spike of tiny white flowers grows at the tip of the stem. The fuzzy spike arches upward and droops at the tip. The plants of this family are found in swamps and along stream banks. Lizard's Tail is representative of this family.

Saururus cernuus L.   Lizard's Tail

A 4 to 6-inch spike of tiny white flowers terminates the jointed succulent stem; with the narrowing tip drooping. Leaves are heart-shaped and 3 to 6 inches long. The plant grows from 1 to 5 feet tall in swamps, marshes and along stream banks throughout Pennsylvania.

June-September

Esther G. Allen

12

ARISTOLOCHIACEAE
Birthwort Family

These are plants of tropical and temperate regions. Flowers are brownish, often growing beneath the heart-shaped leaves. Wild Ginger is representative of this family.

Asarum canadense L. var. *canadense*   Wild Ginger
Indian Ginger

The flowers are 1. 5 inches wide on a short stalk at the junction of the petioles of two leaves. They are dark reddish-brown, cup-shaped, with three pointed, flaring sepals. There are no petals. Flowers are frequently half buried in leaf litter. The leaves range from heart to kidney-shape and are 5 to 6 inches wide on 6 to 12-inch petioles. Flowers and leaves come directly from an aromatic and pungent downy rhizome. Rhizomes were once used medicinally during childbirth and as a substitute for ginger. They are located in shady, moist, rich woods throughout Pennsylvania.

April-May

Virginia A. Phelps

Aristolochia serpentaria L.   Virginia Snakeroot
Birthwort

Located close to the ground, sometimes hidden in leaf litter, are purplish-brown flowers in a curved-pipe shape 0.6 inches long. Crooked wiry stems have alternate leaves, heart-shaped at the base with pointed tips. Virginia Snakeroot was used as a treatment for snakebite and fevers, and as a heart tonic and aphrodisiac. This upright, herbaceous perennial growing up to 2 feet tall is found in rich, dry, upland woods in the southern half of Pennsylvania.

May-June

Esther G. Allen

Aristolochia macrophylla Lam.

Dutchman's Pipe
Pipe-Vine

Purplish-brown three-lobed flowers are curved into a Dutch pipe shape. Heart-shaped leaves are 6 to 8 inches wide along the woody, twining vine. This perennial, fast-growing vine has fertile as well as vegetative shoots, and the vine may reach 100 feet in length. It grows in rich woods and along streams, but is quite rare in southwestern Pennsylvania.

Robert F. Bahl

May-June

NELUMBONACEAE
Lotus Family

These are large aquatic plants with elevated or floating leaves and pale yellow flowers. The receptacle of the flower forms the large, distinctive seed pod. One member of this family is native to North America, the American Lotus, and is representative of this family.

Nelumbo lutea (Willd.) Pers.   American Lotus

The graceful pale yellow flowers are up to 8 inches in diameter, and both flower and foliage are held 1 foot or more above the water surface. Leaves are broadly funnel-shaped with a center stem, and may be 1 to 2 feet in diameter. The plants grow in ponds and slow deep rivers. The greater size as well as the seed-pod distinguishes it from other aquatic plants. The seeds and the submerged tubers are starchy and considered edible. This plant occurs in a few scattered sites in Pennsylvania and should be protected.

July-September

Esther G. Allen

NYMPHAEACEAE
Water Lily Family

Single flowers are carried on non-leafy stalks. Leaves are very broad and may float on or be carried above the water. These are herbaceous, perennial water plants with submerged horizontal rhizomes. The Fragrant Water Lily is representative of this family.

Nymphaea odorata Ait.   Fragrant Water-lily

This aquatic plant has numerous tapering white petals and many yellow stamens. The flower has a sweet scent, and may be up to 5 inches across. The floating leaves are purplish beneath, and are 4 to 12 inches in diameter. Petal size, flower center, and floating leaves distinguish this plant from the similar looking American Lotus, *Nelumbo lutea* (Willd.) Pers. It grows in ponds and quiet waterways mainly in eastern Pennsylvania.

June-September

John Kuehn

Nuphar lutea (L.) Sibth. & Smith — Yellow Pond-lily / Spatterdock

This aquatic plant has yellow flowers that are 1.5 to 3.5 inches across, usually with six yellow sepals and numerous reddish petals below the central disk. Floating leaves are usually 4 to 16 inches across with a triangular sinus. Often growing in large patches, this plant may be found in ponds and slow streams in most of Pennsylvania except the southwest.

May-October

Emily Johnson

Esther G. Allen

17

CABOMBACEAE
Water-shield Family

Aquatic, perennial plants make up this family. The submerged stems are covered with a gelatinous film and have alternate, floating leaves. Flowers occur singly from leaf axils and may be white, yellow or purple. Water Shield is representative of this family.

———————

Brasenia schreberi J. F. Gmel.   Water Shield

The conspicuous identifying feature of this water plant is its floating, oval leaves attached to the stem in the center. The dull purple flower is 0.75-inch across. This aquatic plant grows in ponds and sluggish streams in scattered sites across northern and eastern Pennsylvania.

June-September

Robert F. Bahl

18

RANUNCULACEAE
Buttercup Family

There are many flower forms in this large and interesting family. Flower colors range from white, yellow, pink to red, and blue to violet. Leaves are usually alternate and may be simple or compound. Both annual and perennial plants are represented. The Common Buttercup is representative of this family.

Ranunculus acris L.

Common Buttercup
Tall Buttercup

Flowers are 1 inch across and have overlapping shiny yellow petals. Leaves are three-lobed and deeply cut. The erect, hairy stems are up to 3 feet tall. It is common in wet places throughout Pennsylvania.

May-September

Mary Joy Haywood

Ted J. Griesz

Aconitum uncinatum L.   Blue Monkshood

The distinctive blue flower has a hood-shaped upper sepal that covers the 1-inch wide flower. Several flowers grow from the upper leaf axils. The leaves are deeply divided into three lobes and are 3 to 4 inches wide. This is a perennial herb with a weak stem 2 to 4 feet tall. It is not common but may be found in woods or ravines in a few sites in western Pennsylvania.

August-October

Virginia A. Phelps

Actea pachipoda Ell.   White Baneberry
    syn. *Actea alba* (L.) P. Mill.   Doll's Eyes

    The oblong flower head has four to ten tightly spaced flowers that are white
with narrow petals and numerous stamens. The compound leaves have five
leaflets that are sharply toothed. The fruit is a cluster of white berries on thick
red stems, each having a dark "eye." The name "Doll's Eyes" was a fanciful
name given by little girls who used them for their homemade dolls. This is a
perennial herb growing 1 to 2 feet tall, and is found in rich woods throughout
Pennsylvania.

May-June

Virginia A. Phelps

21

Robert F. Bahl

Actaea rubra (Ait.) Willd.

Red Baneberry

White flowers 0.5-inch across form a rounded cluster. Each flower has four to eight petals and four or five sepals. This perennial herb has leaves divided into five sharply toothed leaflets that are pubescent on the veins beneath. Fruits are red berries. It is not common in Pennsylvania, but may be found in some of the northern tier counties in woods and thickets.

May-June

Esther G. Allen

Anemone canadensis L.

Canada Anemone

Showy white sepals on the 1 to 1.5-inch flowers are on long-branched stalks above the sessile leaves. The latter are 3 to 9 inches wide and three-lobed, each with several teeth. This perennial herb grows 1 to 2 feet tall in moist wooded areas. It is not very common in Pennsylvania.

May-July

Anemone quinquefolia L.

Wood Anemone
Windflower

Five white sepals surround the numerous stamens and pistils of the 1 to 1.5-inch flower. The deeply cut leaves have three to five leaflets on the stem. This herbaceous perennial grows 1 to 2 feet tall in moist woods throughout Pennsylvania.

April-June

Virginia A. Phelps

Anemone virginiana L.

Thimbleweed
Tall Anemone

Several white or greenish flowers top long hairy stalks that branch above the leaves. The "thimble"-shaped flower center forms an elongated fruit. Three-lobed leaves are hairy, lobed, and toothed, and are 1 to 7 inches wide. This erect perennial grows 2 to 3 feet tall in dry woods or meadows throughout Pennsylvania.

July-August

Robert F. Bahl

23

Robert F. Bahl

Aquilegia canadensis L.

Wild Columbine

The flowers are red and yellow, 1 to 2 inches long, and the drooping head nods in the slightest breeze. Scalloped, wedge-shaped leaflets comprise the compound leaves that are 4 to 6 inches wide. This perennial herb grows 1 to 2 feet high in rocky woods throughout Pennsylvania.

April-July

Caltha palustris L. var. *palustris*   Marsh Marigold

Bright yellow flowers have five to nine sepals and are 1 to 1.5 inches across. Shiny leaves are heart or kidney-shaped, 2 to 7 inches broad. The thick hollow stems grow 1 to 2 feet high, very often near standing or flowing water, throughout Pennsylvania.

April-June

Richard McDermot

Cimicifuga racemosa (L.) Nutt.

Black Cohosh
Black Snakeroot

A tall branching spire of creamy white flowers has feathery clumps of stamens and a single pistil. Tapering spires may be 1 to 3 feet tall. Leaves are divided then subdivided into leaflets in threes. This perennial herb grows 3 to 9 feet tall, and may be found in wet or dry woods throughout Pennsylvania.

June-September

Esther G. Allen

Clematis occidentalis (Hornem.) syn. *Clematis verticillaris.*

Purple Clematis.
Purple Virgin's Bower

The purple to blue flowers are very downy and 2 to 4 inches across. They form at the junction of opposite compound leaves. Leaves are divided into three leaflets that are mostly entire and pointed. This perennial woody-stemmed vine grows 3 to 10 feet long in rocky woods and thickets mostly in eastern and central Pennsylvania.

May-June

Esther G. Allen

25

Attractive bell-shaped flowers about 1 inch long have four thick pinkish-purple sepals that curve outward at the tips. Fruits are clusters of feathery plumes. Opposite leaves are divided into three to seven leaflets. This perennial vine climbs over other vegetation in woods and thickets and is rare in Pennsylvania.

May-August

Phyllis T. Monk

Esther G. Allen

Clematis virginiana L.

Virgin's Bower
Old Man's Beard

A cluster of white four-sepaled pistillate flowers, 0.75 to 1.25 inches broad, grows from the leaf axils of this climbing vine. In fall, the flowers form a cluster of many feathery plumes about 3 inches across. Three pointed, toothed leaflets comprise the stem leaves. This perennial vine grows over other vegetation in thickets and woods, and is common in Pennsylvania.

Robert F. Bahl

July-September

Coptis trifolia (L.) Salisb. ssp. *groenlandica* (Oeder) Hulten

Goldthread

Flowers are solitary with five white sepals surrounding five smaller petals. The deep green leaves have three wedge-shaped toothed leaflets. This is an evergreen perennial from 3 to 6 inches high. The distinguishing characteristic is the root system of numerous yellow strands. This plant is found in damp, cool, wooded areas and bogs through-out Pennsylvania.

May-July

Robert F. Bahl

Delphinium exaltatum Ait.

Tall Larkspur

A terminal cluster of 0.5 to 0.75-inch blue or white flowers tops the stem, which has numerous three to five lobed leaves. Tall Larkspur is a slender plant growing 2 to over 6 feet tall. This plant grows in open woods and rocky slopes over 1,000 feet, and is very rare in Pennsylvania.

July-September

Werner E. Buker

Delphinium tricorne Michx.   Dwarf Larkspur

The 1-inch flowers may be bright blue, purple or white. The spur extends upward behind the flower. Flowers occur in a loose raceme at the top of the stem. The leaves are mostly basal with lobed margins that are deeply cut. Dwarf Larkspur has a 1 to 2-foot stem, and the plant is found in woods and on slopes throughout western Pennsylvania.

April-May

Scott J. Shriver

Hepatica nobilis P.Mill.   Round-lobed Hepatica
   var. *obtusa* (Pursh) Steyerm.

A tuft of several white, pink or blue 0.75-inch flowers grows from the base of the plant on densely hairy stalks. The three-lobed leaves have rounded tips and are purplish-green. Young leaves have several tiny lobes and are bright green. This perennial plant grows 4 to 9 inches tall in rich moist woods throughout Pennsylvania except in the northwest corner.

March-May

Esther G. Allen

Hepatica nobilis P.Mill var. *acuta* (Pursh) Steyerm.

Sharp-lobed Hepatica

Similar to the Round-lobed Hepatica, the sharply pointed leaves of this plant is its distinguishing characteristic. Flowers are white, pink or blue, leaves are purplish-green and the plant grows 4 to 9 inches high. It is found in rich moist woods throughout Pennsylvania except in the southeastern counties.

March-April

Esther G. Allen

29

Hydrastis canadensis L.

Goldenseal
Yellowroot

The solitary 1-inch flower head at the top of the stem consists of twelve or more clustered stamens and pistils. The plant has three leaves, two on the stem and one at the base. The leaves are palmately lobed and toothed and 4 to 8 inches broad. This perennial herb grows 8 to 15 inches high in rich, moist woods, and is now uncommon in Pennsylvania due to medicinal collecting.

April-May

Virginia A. Phelps

Ranunculus abortivus L. var. *abortivus*

Kidney-leaf Buttercup
Small-flowered Crowfoot

Yellow flowers 0.25-inch across are borne at the top of spreading stalks. Basal leaves are three-lobed and divided. Stem leaves are variable. This biennial plant grows 6 to 24 inches tall in woods and damp areas and is common in Pennsylvania.

April-August

Virginia A. Phelps

Ranunculus ficaria L.   Lesser Celandine
                                                           Introduced

   Shiny yellow flowers consist of eight to ten petals. Leaves are cordate to
ovate. The plant grows 2 to 8 inches high from fibrous roots. This herbaceous
perennial has become naturalized in flood plains and meadows primarily in eastern
counties and a few areas in southwestern Pennsylvania.

                                                           April-June

Mary Joy Haywood

Ranunculus flabellaris Raf.   Yellow Water-buttercup

   This aquatic plant has yellow flowers 0.2 to 0.5 inch across on stout flower
stalks. The submerged leaves are finely divided and the above-water leaves are
divided into three to five lobes. It grows in ponds and quiet water but is not common
in Pennsylvania.

                                                           May-June

Esther G. Allen

Ranunculus septentrionalis Poir.

Northern Swamp Buttercup
Marsh Buttercup

Yellow flowers 0.5 to 1.5 inches across are on stalks that arise from the creeping stem. Leaves are three-lobed and each lobe is further divided and toothed. Stems are hollow and form runners from 1 to 3 feet long. It is found in swamps and moist areas throughout Pennsylvania.

April-July

Virginia A. Phelps

Thalictrum dioicum L.   Early Meadow Rue

The greenish flowers have many drooping stamens with yellow anthers. Inconspicuous pistillate flowers are borne on separate plants. Many scallop-edged leaflets make up the bluish-green leaves. This perennial plant grows 1 to 2 feet tall in moist woods, and is found throughout Pennsylvania.

April-May

Robert F. Bahl

Thalictrum pubescens Pursh. syn. *Thalictrum polygamum* Muhl.

Tall Meadow Rue
Late Meadow Rue

Four to 12-inch clusters of pistillate and staminate flowers are whitish or purplish in sprays at the top of the plant. Compound leaves have many oval three-lobed leaflets. This perennial grows from 3 to 8 feet tall in swampy areas and along roadsides throughout Pennsylvania.

July-September

Robert F. Bahl

Thalictrum thalictroides (L.) Eams & B.Boivin

Rue Anemone

White or pinkish flowers are 0.5 to 1 inch wide. Long-stalked leaflets are in three groups of three at the base of the plant, and form a whorl below the flowers. This perennial herb grows 4 to 10 inches high in open woods throughout Pennsylvania.

March-May

Phyllis T. Monk

33

Trautvetteria caroliniensis (Walt.) Vail.   Tassel Rue

Flowers are 0.2 to 0.5-inch across and consist of many white stamens surrounded by four inconspicuous sepals. Leaves are palmately cut with five to eleven deep lobes. This perennial grows in moist places with only two locations in southwestern Pennsylvania.

June-July

Virginia A. Phelps

Trollius laxus Salisb.   Globe Flower

    Five to seven white or pale yellow cup-shaped sepals surround a center of numerous yellow pistils and stamens. Leaves are palmate; the upper two sessile, surrounding the stem. This is a native perennial 4 to 20 inches high. This plant is very rare but may be found in swamps and wet woods at several sites in eastern and western Pennsylvania.

April-June

Esther G. Allen

BERBERIDACEAE
Barberry Family

Members of this family have flowers with stamens grouped below a single central pistil. Overlapping sepals and petals within the flower bud distinguish several species that appear to be dissimilar. Fruit may be a capsule or a berry. These plants may be woody or herbaceous. The Mayapple is a representative of this family.

Podophyllum peltatum L.

Mayapple
Mandrake

The familiar umbrella-shaped leaves of Mayapple are a welcome sign that spring has arrived. The foot-wide leaf is carried on a central stem that is 1 to 1.5 feet tall. First year plants have an unbranched stem, while a second year plant has two terminal branches from which a waxy white flower emerges on a short stalk. The flower is 2 inches across and is fragrant. The flower later matures into a pale, yellow-green "apple," which is sweet and edible only when it is solid yellow. The plant often grows in large groups in moist, rich woodlands throughout Pennsylvania.

April-June

Esther G. Allen

Esther G. Allen

Caulophyllum thalictroides (L.) Michx.   Blue Cohosh

Before the leaves fully open, the 0.5-inch flowers of this plant bloom in clusters at the tips of the stems. The six tiny petal-like bracts are yellowish to rich maroon and the six tiny rounded petals surround the yellow inner floral parts. As the plant emerges from the ground, the foliage and stems are bluish purple, later becoming green as full height is reached. Bluish berries follow the mature flowers. This plant grows 1 to 3 feet tall, and may be found in rich moist woods throughout Pennsylvania.

April-June

Esther G. Allen

Jeffersonia diphylla (L.) Pers.   Twinleaf

The deeply divided leaf distinguishes this plant from other early spring plants having white flowers. The leaf is borne on an 8 to10-inch stalk. On a separate stalk, the single white flower has eight petals. It appears similar to Bloodroot, *Sanguinaria canadensis* L. After blooming, the foliage grows to 16 inches tall. The flower matures into a 1 to 2-inch capsule that has a conical, hinged top. The swaying capsule spreads seed a foot or more from the plant. This beautiful plant commemorates President Jefferson and grows in the areas where he explored as a naturalist. Twinleaf grows in rich woodlands in a few scattered counties of Pennsylvania.

April-May

Phyllis T. Monk

MENISPERMACEAE
Moonseed Family

These plants are woody vines with large alternating leaves. The plants are male or female with tiny flowers that occur in spreading groups where leaves join the stem. The fruit is a round single-seeded drupe. The Canada Moonseed is representative of this family.

Menispermum canadense L.   Canada Moonseed

One to 2-inch clusters of tiny white flowers grow in leaf axils near the end of stems. The plants are dioecious, and the female flowers mature into black fruits that may be mistaken for wild grapes. This woody-stemmed vine has unlobed and shallowly-lobed leaves from 5 to 8 inches across. Leaf stalks attach above the base of the leaf, and often twine around objects. The vine lacks tendrils. This vine usually grows in moist woods and along stream banks in some areas of northwest Pennsylvania.

June-July

Robert F. Bahl

39

PAPAVERACEAE
Poppy Family

This is a group of mostly herbaceous annual, biennial, or perennial plants, having regular flowers with stamens attached below the central pistil. Plant sap may be yellow, red, or milky white. Petals are in fours and the fruit is a capsule. Bloodroot is representative of this family.

Sanguinaria canadensis L.   Bloodroot

One of the earliest plants to bloom in the spring, Bloodroot has eight or twelve petals arranged in a square outline, with four longer "corner" petals and four or eight shorter petals between. The flower may be from 1.5 to 2.5 inches across, on a 3 to 6-inch high stem. Named for the red sap in the fibrous root, a slight pinkish color shows in the veins of the emerging leaves. Fully developed leaves are 6 to 12 inches broad, palmately lobed, green above and whitish beneath. These plants are found in patches in rich woodland soil throughout Pennsylvania.

March-May

Edith R. Mock

Chelidonium majus L.

Celandine
Introduced

This leafy, 2-foot high plant has 0.5 to 0.75-inch wide yellow flowers. There are two sepals below the four petals that surround the numerous stamens. The flowers mature into smooth, long, upright capsules. The leaves are divided into many incised lobes, and may be from 4 to 8 inches long. This common biennial plant may be found in damp soil along roadsides and waste places throughout Pennsylvania.

April-August

Esther G. Allen

Papaver rhoeas L.

Erect, branching stems from 1 to 3 feet tall bear scarlet flowers 2 to 4 inches across. There are four rounded petals, and a capsule-like ovary surrounded by numerous stamens. Hairy leaves are lobed and have toothed margins. The stem is covered with bristly hairs. This plant is a native of Europe, and grows in waste places in a few scattered counties of southeast and central Pennsylvania.

May-October

Robert F. Bahl

FUMARIACEAE
Bleeding-heart Family

This family has irregular-appearing flowers that are bilaterally symmetrical. Plants have watery sap, finely dissected leaves, and the flowers are arranged along one or both sides of a separate stem. Dutchman's Breeches is representative of this family.

Dicentra cucullaria (L.) Bernh.   Dutchman's Breeches

Arising on separate stems, as many as ten flowers have the shape of white and yellow "breeches." Bright green, finely divided leaves grow in 5 to 9-inch high masses. A clump of pointed pinkish underground tubers, beneath the base of the plant, store food for future growth. This plant is present on hillsides in rich woods throughout Pennsylvania.

April-May

Phyllis T. Monk

43

Adlumia fungosa (Ait.) Greene

Allegheny Vine

This slender biennial vine spreads over other plants by its delicate coiling leaf stalks, and may reach 10 to 12 feet in length. The leaves are finely divided into three sets of leaflets. Flowers are long and slender, with four joined, pale pink or white petals. Groups of flowers droop from leaf axils. This vine grows in woods and thickets, on rocky ledges, and mountainous terrain that is scattered over most of Pennsylvania.

June-October

Corydalis flavula Raf.

Yellow Corydalis

One-quarter inch yellow flowers have flaring, toothed upper lips. The small leaves are typical of this family, and the plant grows from 6 to 14 inches high. It is a fairly common biennial found in rich, moist woods, in the southern half of Pennsylvania.

April-May

Corydalis sempervirens (L.) Pers.

Pale Corydalis
Rock Harlequin

    The pink and yellow flower has a distinct bulbous base. The 0.5-inch flowers cluster at the top of a leafy stem and in the leaf axils. The leaves are finely divided and have a whitish bloom covering the underside. This somewhat rare perennial grows from 0.5 inch to 2 feet high in rich, moist soil, often among rocks, throughout Pennsylvania.

May-September

Virginia A. Phelps

Dicentra canadensis (Goldie) Walp.

Squirrel Corn

    The white flowers are carried on pinkish stems and are heart-shaped. The leaves are bluish-green and have the typical form for this family. The name describes a rounded, yellow tuber beneath the stems slightly underground. The plant blooms before the nearby trees leaf out, and dies back in three weeks after blooming. It lives on rich, wooded hillsides throughout Pennsylvania.

April-May

Phyllis T. Monk

45

Dicentra eximia (Ker-Gawl.) Torr.   Wild Bleeding Heart

    The pink flowers are about 0.5-inch long and are in a cluster atop a separate stem. This smaller biennial plant is similar to the cultivated Bleeding Heart, *Dicentra spectabilis*. It grows from 10 inches to 2 feet in height. This rare plant grows at higher elevations along the Allegheny Mountains in moist, rich soil in rocky areas of Pennsylvania.

May-August

Virginia A. Phelps

Fumaria officinalis L.

Fumitory
Introduced

    The pink flowers are less than 0.5-inch long and have a crimson tip. Very finely divided gray-green leaves distinguish this plant from other pink-flowered members of this family. A climbing native of Europe, this plant may reach 3 feet in height. It can be found in waste places in southeastern Pennsylvania.

May-August

Robert F. Bahl

HAMEMELIDACEAE
Witch-hazel Family

This family consists of woody shrubs or trees. Two species occur in Pennsylvania; the shrub Witch-hazel is one and the other is the Sweet Gum tree. Fruits are woody capsules. The Witch-hazel is representative of this family.

———————

Hamemelis virginiana L.

Witch-hazel

Bright yellow flowers with four narrow twisted petals, 0.75-inch long, are in leaf axils near the end of branches. Leaves are 3 to 6 inches long, elliptical, alternate, and with wavy-toothed margins. This is an aromatic shrub 10 to 15 feet tall with smooth or scaly bark. Twigs are slender and zigzag. Leaf buds have no scales. Fruit is a two-valved capsule with two black shiny seeds. The capsule bursts violently when dried and casts seeds up to 50 feet away. An extract of this plant is soothing to the skin and is used in lotions. This shrub grows in moist soil in woodlands and is found throughout Pennsylvania.

Robert F. Bahl

October-November

Phyllis T. Monk

URTICACEAE
Nettle Family

Inconspicuous greenish flowers are found in the axils of usually opposite toothed leaves. Some plants have stinging hairs and some do not. These plants are located in damp woods, in ditches, and along streams. The Stinging Nettle is representative of this family.

Urtica dioica L. ssp. *dioica*   Stinging Nettle
                                                     Introduced

Tiny green flowers grow in drooping or spreading clusters in the axils of the upper leaves. The flowers may be staminate or pistillate, usually on separate plants. Leaves that are opposite, toothed, and heart-shaped are covered with bristly, stinging hairs. The stem is also armed with stinging hairs. The burning sensation which results, may be relieved by rubbing on the sap of crushed Jewelweed, *Impatiens* sp., which often grows nearby. Plants grow 2 to 4 feet high in wet waste places throughout Pennsylvania.

June-September

Jay B. Brown

48

PHYTOLACCACEAE
Pokeweed Family

These large branching plants have entire leaves and reddish stems. Flowers are borne in racemes. Fruits are juicy black berries. These plants are found in clearings and along roadsides. Pokeweed is representative of this family.

———◦•••◦———

Phytolacca americana L.

Pokeweed
Pokeberry

Upright racemes of white or pinkish flowers are at the ends of the many-branched stems. Later the heavy raceme of black shiny berries droops. Alternate leaves are 5 to 23 inches long and tapered at both ends. Stems are reddish and succulent, growing 6 to 12 feet high. Plants are extremely toxic except for the very young green shoots. A natural ink was derived from the juice of the berries. Pokeweed may be found in wet places, clearings, and coastal dunes across Pennsylvania.

July-September

Phyllis T. Monk   Robert F. Bahl

CACTACEAE
Cactus Family

Plants in this family have flattened, oval, fleshy stems with spines. Many-petaled flowers grow directly from the upper stem, and mature into a pulpy, edible fruit. The Prickly Pear is representative of this family.

Phyllis T. Monk

Opuntia humifusa (Raf.) Raf.

Prickly Pear Cactus

The yellow flower is 2 to 3.5 inches across and often has a star-shaped center. It remains closed except in bright sunlight. The rounded, flattened stems have tufts of bristles and a single spine in each tuft. It grows in low clumps that spread from fibrous roots in rocky or sandy soil, and is found in a few southern counties of Pennsylvania.

June-August

Esther G. Allen

Lychnis coronaria (L.) Desr.

Mullein-Pink
Rose Campion
Introduced

A few crimson flowers are scattered at the tips of densely white-wooly stems. The white-wooly basal leaves are 2 to 4 inches long. Stem leaves are similar but smaller. This perennial grows on sturdy stems 15 to 32 inches high. It has escaped garden cultivation and is found along roadsides and waste places primarily in the eastern counties of Pennsylvania.

June-August

Robert F. Bahl

Lychnis flos-cuculi L.

Ragged-robin
Cuckoo Flower
Introduced

The deep pink or white petals are deeply four-cleft and the flowers are 0.75 to 1-inch wide. Elongated leaves are paired along the 1 to 3-foot tall stem. This perennial is found in waste places in eastern Pennsylvania.

June-July

Virginia A. Phelps

55

Robert K. Grubbs

Saponaria officinalis L.

Bouncing Bet
Soapwort
Introduced

Fragrant pink to white flowers are in dense clusters at the top of a 1 to 2-foot stout stem. Lance-ovate leaves are strongly ribbed. Plant juices will form a soap-like lather. This poisonous plant may form dense patches and is common in waste places and along roadsides across Pennsylvania.

July-September

Esther G. Allen

Silene alba (Mill.) Krause

Evening Lychnis
White Campion
Introduced

The white or pink flower opens in the evening and closes in the forenoon. It is 1 inch wide with a calyx more or less inflated when aged. The plant is 1 to 2 feet high and pubescent. Leaves are ovate to lance-oblong and 1 to 3 inches long. It is a biennial and often dioecious, and is located in fields and waste places in Pennsylvania.

June-September

Silene caroliniana Walt.   Wild Pink
       ssp. *pensylvanica* (Michx.) Clausen

Terminal clusters of pink to white flowers top the 4 to 10-inch plant. The tubular calyx is long and narrow, and petals are only slightly indented. Basal leaves are lanceolate. This perennial plant arises from a deep fleshy taproot, and grows on rocky banks and edges of woods throughout Pennsylvania.

April-June

Virginia A. Phelps

Silene nivea (Nutt.) Otth.   Snowy Campion

Five scarcely-notched white petals spread from a bell-shaped calyx. Attached at leaf axils, the flowers are about 1 inch wide. Oblong-lanceolate leaves are paired along the 8 to 12-inch high stem. This perennial plant is not common. There are a few sites in western and southeastern Pennsylvania in woods and shaded ravines.

June-August

Esther G. Allen

Esther G. Allen

Silene stellata (L.) Ait.

Starry Campion

Petals are white and deeply fringed, and the flowers are 0.75-inch wide in a loose inflorescence. Middle leaves are in whorls of four and are ovate-lanceolate, 2 to 3 inches long. The plant grows from 1 to 3 feet tall. It is found in open woods and clearings, at higher elevations throughout Pennsylvania.

July-September

Robert F. Bahl

Silene virginica L.

Fire Pink

Brilliant red flowers 1 to 1.5 inches across are in a loose cluster. Petals are narrow and cleft at the tips. Two to four pairs of stem leaves are oblong-lanceolate. This perennial plant grows 6 to 20 inches tall from a basal rosette of oblong leaves. It may be found on rocky slopes and open woods mostly in western Pennsylvania.

April-June

Hypericum punctatum L.

Spotted St. John's Wort

Very similar to Common St. John's Wort, this plant is slightly shorter. Flowers are more heavily spotted and leaves have black dots. It is common in open fields, thickets and damp places throughout Pennsylvania.

June-September

Robert F. Bahl

Hypericum pyramidatum Ait.   Great St. John's Wort

Five bright yellow petals surround the spray of stamens. Several 1 to 2 inch- flowers are at the tips of branching stems. Pointed oval leaves clasp the stem and are 1.5 to 2.5 inches long. This perennial grows 2 to 5 feet tall in low meadows and along stream banks, and is widely scattered in eastern and western counties of Pennsylvania.

June-August

Jay B. Brown

67

Hypericum prolificum L.   Shrubby St. John's Wort

Golden yellow flowers grow in leaf axils as well as the tips of the multi-branched stems. Leaves are elongated and tufts of tiny leaves grow in the axils of larger leaves. This perennial shrub grows 2 to 6 feet tall at the margin of swamps, in old fields, and on rocky slopes, and is widely distributed at lower elevations in Pennsylvania.

July-September

Robert F. Bahl

Triadenum virginicum (L.) Raf.   Marsh St. John's Wort
    syn. *Hypericum virginicum* L.

The pink flower of Marsh St. John's Wort is 0.5 to 0.75-inch wide and opens in the early evening. Leaves are sessile, oblong and 1 to 3 inches wide. This perennial grows 1 to 2 feet tall and the whole plant may have a reddish cast. It is found in bogs, swamps, and ditches in scattered locations in Pennsylvania.

July-August

Robert F. Bahl

MALVACEAE
Mallow Family

A typical flower of this family is the Hollyhock or Hibiscus with five showy petals and a central column of five fused stigmas and five fused stamens. Plants are herbaceous or woody and include the cultivated cotton plant. Marshmallow, *Althaea officinalis* L., which has a perennial root, yields the original mucilaginous paste of the marshmallow. Musk Mallow is representative of this family.

Malva moschata L.

Musk Mallow
Introduced

This is a 1 to 2 foot tall plant with showy pink or white flowers, and sturdy stems. The leaves are finely cut into five to seven lobes. Basal leaves are broad and rounded. This is a perennial native of Europe, and grows along roadsides and in fields throughout Pennsylvania.

June-September

Esther G. Allen

Abutilon theophrasti Medic.

Velvet leaf
Indian Mallow
Introduced

Small yellow flowers 0.6 to 1 inch wide are found in the upper leaf axils. The velvety leaves are 4 to 10 inches long and have a pointed heart shape. The plant grows from 3 to 5 feet tall in waste places that are scattered throughout Pennsylvania, particularly in the southeast.

July-October

Virginia A. Phelps

Althea officinalis L.

Marsh-mallow
Introduced

 The pink five-petaled flowers have purple-tipped stamens in a fused column. Flowers grow terminally or in upper leaf axils and are 1 to 1.5-inch across. The broadly ovate or obtuse leaves are alternate and toothed, often with three shallow lobes. The velvety leaf is covered with whitish down and has raised veins on the paler underside. This European perennial was cultivated for the mucilaginous material in the roots, and was used in making marsh-mallows. It grows in salt marshes or inland in ditches in widely scattered sites in Pennsylvania.

Phyllis T. Monk

July-September

Hibiscus moscheutos L.
 syn. *Hibiscus palustris* L.

Swamp Rose Mallow

 A shrub 3 to 7 feet tall, Swamp Rose Mallow has 4 to 6-inch wide pink flowers that resemble a garden Hibiscus. The young stems and lower surfaces of leaves are covered with a whitish down. Leaves are 0.25 to 1 inch long, broad and pointed, and sometimes shallowly three-lobed. This plant may be found in marshy areas in fresh or brackish water, and is uncommon in Pennsylvania.

August-September

Esther G. Allen

Hibiscus trionum L.   Flower-of-an-hour
                                                                    Introduced

The 1 to 2-inch flowers have five pale yellow petals with a deep purple center. The flower buds are broadly inflated. The plant's name describes the way the flowers quickly wilt after blooming. The leaves are three-parted with a longer center leaflet. Each leaflet is very narrow with rounded teeth. Stems and leaves are covered with tiny hairs. This plant is found in southern Pennsylvania.

July-September

Esther G. Allen

71

Malva neglecta Wallr.

Common Mallow
Cheeses
Introduced

This sprawling plant has 0.5-inch pale pink flowers in the upper leaf axils. The rounded leaves appear wrinkled with scalloped margins. Its name "Cheeses" refers to the round flat shape of the fruit. Native to Eurasia and North Africa it grows in uncultivated areas throughout Pennsylvania.

April-October

Robert F. Bahl

Malva sylvestris L.

High Mallow

Flowers are in clusters at the tip of stems. The five indented white petals have deep red veins radiating from the flower center. The ivy-like leaves have five to seven lobes. This plant is a European biennial that has escaped cultivation and grows from 1 to 3 feet tall in moist ditches. It is not abundant but is scattered throughout Pennsylvania.

June-August

Robert F. Bahl

SARRACENIACEAE
Pitcher-plant Family

Plants in this family have leaves adapted for attracting and capturing insects. Their watery habitat lacks soil, limiting the availability of nitrogen compounds necessary for plant life. Their insect prey provide this necessary nutrient. These plants are able to grow in places that many other plants find inhospitable. Pitcher-plant is a perennial with a single nodding flower, and is representative of this family.

Sarracenia purpurea L.   Pitcher-plant

The name is descriptive of the pitcher-like form of the leaves. They are light green, often heavily veined in red, and lined with stiff downward-pointing hairs that help prevent the escape of their insect prey. Leaves may be from 4 to 12 inches long, and hold a supply of water. Deep red pendant flowers top the 1 to 2-foot flower stalks that arise from the center of the plant. Insects that become trapped in the leaf are digested enzymatically. Pitcher-plant grows only in sphagnum bogs that are scattered across Pennsylvania.

May-July

Virginia A. Phelps

Virginia A. Phelps

73

DROSERACEAE
Sundew Family

The Greek term for "dew" is *"droseros"* and refers to the shining drops of digestive fluid secreted by the leaf glands. The leaves of these plants attract insects, which supply necessary nitrogen compounds lacking in their watery habitat. New leaves arise from a central rosette, and uncoil in a manner similar to fern fronds. Flowers are grouped on a single thin stalk and open only in the brightest sunlight. The Round-leaved Sundew is representative of this family.

Drosera rotundifolia L.   Round-leaved Sundew

Tiny rounded leaves covered with glistening reddish hairs have narrow stalks and are from 0.25 to 0.5-inch across. The five-petaled flowers are at the top of a curving stalk, and open only in the brightest sunlight. The whole plant is usually less than 3 inches in diameter. Like all Sundews, it is insectivorous capturing and digesting tiny insects on the leaf hairs. This plant is common in sphagnum bogs across Pennsylvania.

June-August

Robert K. Grubbs

Drosera intermedia Hayne

Spatulate-leaved Sundew

Like the more common Round-leaved Sundew, *Drosera rotundifolia,* L., this plant has leaves adapted for attracting and capturing small insects. The leaves are slender, widening at the tip, and may be 0.5 to 1.5 inches long. The leaf is covered with short reddish hairs that secrete a digestive fluid. As many as twenty five-petaled white flowers may appear on a slender 2 to 8-inch stalk that arises from the center of the leaf rosette. This plant lives in sphagnum bogs in eastern Pennsylvania.

Phyllis T. Monk

June-August

Drosera linearis Goldie

Slender-leaved Sundew

The distinctive feature of the Slender-leaved Sundew is the filament-like leaf 0.5 to 2.5 inches long. It is adapted for catching insects with its tiny reddish hairs that secrete digestive juices. The flower stalk is often shorter than the leaves, and holds a single white flower, and grows in sphagnum bogs across Pennsylvania.

June-August

Phyllis T. Monk

75

CISTACEAE
Rockrose Family

This is a family of low-growing herbaceous or shrub-like plants with narrow, pointed leaves. The early flowers may be yellow or pink with five petals that soon drop off, and later inconspicuous flowers develop without petals. Frostweed is representative of this family.

Helianthemum canadense (L.) Michx.   Frostweed
                                                        Rockrose

Bright yellow five-petaled flowers are about 0.75 to 1.5 inches across. They open in sunlight and last one day. Alternate leaves are 0.5 to 1.2 inches long. The stem is hairy and erect. The name "Frostweed" comes from the ice crystals that form on the lower stem in late fall. This plant grows in dry, sandy soil mostly in eastern Pennsylvania.

May-June

Werner E. Buker

VIOLACEAE
Violet Family

Flowers in this family may be blue to purple, yellow or white, with five petals. Leaves may be deeply lobed or almost entire, often broad and pointed. In addition to the showy flowers, violets produce inconspicuous cleistogamous flowers that are very fertile. To be confident in identifying a violet, it is helpful to become familiar with some family characteristics such as; size and position of the spur, whether the flower stalk arises at the base of the plant or from the main stem, colors or markings on the flower, hairiness, presence of stipules, and leaf forms. Representative of the family in blue is the Marsh Blue Violet, in white is the Canada Violet, and in yellow is the Smooth Yellow Violet.

Viola cucullata Ait.   Marsh Blue Violet

Flowers are blue-violet to white, 0.75-inch long on very long slender stems; upper and lower petals are darker in the center. Cleistogamous flowers are numerous with green capsules. Flowers and leaf stems are separate, with the flower stems usually taller than the leaf stems. Leaves are 3.5 inches wide and the bases are curled inward. This herbaceous perennial grows 5 to 10 inches high arising from a rhizome. Normal habitats are marshy areas, springs, and bogs throughout Pennsylvania.

April-June

Robert F. Bahl

Viola canadensis L. var. *canadensis*   Canada Violet

    White flowers are 0.5 to 0.75-inch across and the petals are tinged with purple on the underside. The spurred petal is yellow at the base and is sparingly veined with purple. Flowers grow on pedicels that arise from the stem. Stipules are small. This perennial plant grows 6 to 16 inches high from a short woody rhizome. It is common in moist, open woods and blooms later than most other violet species, and can be found in the northern and western counties of Pennsylvania.

April-July

Esther G. Allen   Phyllis T. Monk

Viola eriocarpa Schwein.
   syn. *Viola pensylvanica* Michx.

Smooth Yellow Violet
Pennsylvania Violet

    Similar to the Downy Yellow Violet, *Viola pubescens* Ait., the leaves and stems are smooth, and there may be one to five basal leaves. Stipules at the nodes are untoothed. This plant may hybridize with the Downy Yellow Violet. This perennial plant grows 4 to 12 inches high, and is common in moist, open woods and meadows throughout Pennsylvania.

April-June

Virginia A. Phelps

79

Hybanthus concolor (T.F.Forst.) Spreng.   Green Violet

Pendulous, small green flowers form in the axils of the leaves. This herbaceous perennial does not resemble the violets except for the pistil structure and the fruit. The plant grows 1 to 3 feet tall; with alternate leaves 2.8 to 4.3 inches long. This plant is not very common and is easily overlooked. This species is found in rich, moist woods and thickets, and is scattered in southern Pennsylvania.

April-June

Virginia A. Phelps

Viola arvensis Murr

European Field Pansy
Introduced

The flower has yellow petals and sepals with purple markings and a short spur. The petals are shorter than the sepals and the flower is 0.4 to 0.7-inch across. Basal leaves are round to ovate with rounded teeth, and stem leaves are oblong to narrowly elliptic. Stipules are foliacious with five to seven segments. The plant grows up to 4 inches high in fields and along roadsides mostly in eastern Pennsylvania and scattered sites elsewhere.

April-September

Phyllis T. Monk

Viola blanda Willd.   Sweet White Violet

The white sweet-smelling flower is 0.5-inch long with the lower petals veined. Upper petals are frequently curled inward at the base. Flowers grow on separate pedicels. Leaves are 1 to 2 inches wide with reddish petioles. The plant grows 3 to 5 inches tall from a slender rhizome. Frequently cleistogamous flowers form in summer on prostrate peduncles. This perennial grows in cool, moist woods and slopes throughout Pennsylvania.

April-May

Virginia A. Phelps

81

Viola conspersa Reichnb.

American Dog Violet
Early Pale Blue Violet

Pale blue flowers with conspicuous spurs, have bearded lateral petals. Flowers grow on pedicels inserted on the stems at the alternately-placed 1.5-inch leaves. Spreading toothed stipules attach at the base of the pedicels. This perennial plant grows from a rhizome in meadows, low shaded areas, and along streams throughout Pennsylvania.

May-July

Virginia A. Phelps

Viola hastata Michx.

Halberd-leaved Violet

Bright yellow flowers have narrow petals, the upper two flushed with purple underneath. Flowers arise from pedicels joined to the stem. Leaves are elongated triangles that whiten as they age. This slightly downy perennial grows 4 to 10 inches high from a white rhizome that often becomes brittle with age. It is found in mountainous areas in dry woods and ravines, primarily in western Pennsylvania.

April-May

Virginia A. Phelps

Viola hirsutula Brainerd   Southern Wood Violet

Flowers are usually reddish purple and held above the leaves on separate pedicels. The three lower petals are white at the base. The two lateral petals are bearded; the lower petal is veined and not as bearded. Leaves are 0.75 to 2 inches wide. This species is easy to distinguish by the leaves that are pubescent above, smooth and purplish below. This herbaceous perennial grows from a short, thick rhizome. It may be found in dry, open woods or near the edges of woods throughout most of Pennsylvania.

April-May

Virginia A. Phelps

Viola lanceolata L. var. *lanceolata*

Lance-leaved Violet

Delicate white flowers, purple-veined on the lowest petal, grow on separate reddish pedicels. Leaves are 2 to 6 inches long, tapering at each end. This perennial grows 2 to 6 inches high from a slender creeping rhizome that roots at the nodes. This plant is found in bogs, swamps, and marshes, more frequently in eastern than western Pennsylvania.

April-June

Virginia A. Phelps

83

Viola pedata L.   Birdfoot Violet

Flowers are 0.75 to 1.25-inch wide and beardless. The upper two petals are dark violet, the lower three pale blue. Stamens are bright orange. There is also a uniformly pale blue variety. Leaves are 1 to 1.5 inches long, divided into threes, and quite hairy on the margins. This herbaceous perennial grows 4 to 10 inches high on a short erect rhizome. The range of this species is widely scattered, as it requires a shale barrens habitat, and is common in central and southeastern Pennsylvania.

April-June

Virginia A. Phelps

Viola pubescens Ait.   Downy Yellow Violet

The yellow flowers are 0.75-inch long and grow on a pedicel attached to the stem. The lateral petals are bearded and the lower petal is veined. Two to four hairy leaves arise halfway up the hairy stem and are 1 to 1.5 inches long. Stipules at the nodes are toothed. There is a single basal leaf. This downy perennial grows 6 to 17 inches high and arises from a stout rhizome in dry rich woods throughout Pennsylvania.

April-May

Robert F. Bahl

Viola rostrata Pursh   Long-spurred Blue Violet

Pale blue petals are flushed with dark blue at the base, and the 0.5-inch long spur arises almost vertically behind the flower. Flowers grow on pedicels inserted along the stem. Stipules are long and toothed. Heart-shaped leaves are 2 to 4 inches long. A woody rhizome gives rise to a 4 to 8-inch high plant. Preferring rich alkaline soil, this plant grows in rocky woods throughout Pennsylvania.

April-June

Esther G. Allen   85

Viola rotundifolia Michx.   Round-leaved Yellow Violet

Bright yellow flowers are 0.5 inch long. The three lower petals are veined and the lateral petals are bearded. The pedicels are sparsely pubescent. Leaves are heart-shaped at the base and are rounded. This plant also produces cleistogamous flowers in the fall. This perennial arises from a thin rhizome, and grows in rich, cool woods in mountainous areas throughout Pennsylvania.

April-May

Virginia A. Phelps

Viola sagittata Ait.   Northern Downy Violet
    var. *ovata* (Nutt.) Torr. & A.Gray

Violet flowers about 0.8-inch wide are held high above the 0.5 to 3-inch long ovate leaves. Flowers grow on separate pedicels. The entire plant is hairy, and arises from an erect rhizome. This perennial is found in dry fields and open pastures throughout most of Pennsylvania.

April-May

S. G. Shetler

86

Barbarea vulgaris R.Br. var. *vulgaris*

Winter Cress
Yellow Rocket
Introduced

Similar to the Black Mustard, *Brassica nigra* (L.) W.D.J. Koch, this plant grows 1 to 2 feet tall with clusters of yellow, four-petaled flowers at the top of branching stems. Basal leaves have smooth edges and are cut deeply into rounded segments. Along the stem, small, clasping, several-lobed leaves help distinguish this species from others. The upward pointing seed pods may either be held close to the stem or may spread as in the illustration. This common plant grows along roadsides and in moist meadows throughout Pennsylvania.

April-August

Robert F. Bahl

Brassica nigra (L.) W.D.J.Koch

Black Mustard
Introduced

Typical of this family, Black Mustard has a mass of tiny yellow flowers topping a central stem. A distinguishing feature is the way the seedpods clasp the stem below the flowers. Each flower has four petals. The leaves on the stem are smooth and narrow, while the basal leaves are long, broad at the ends, and lobed. The lower leaves are bristly and the margin is finely toothed. These plants are found in scattered locations throughout Pennsylvania.

Common Winter Cress, *Barbarea vulgaris* R. Br. var. *vulgaris*, (Not illustrated), is a similar plant that may be mistaken for Black Mustard. Both of these plants grow 2 to 3 feet tall in waste areas and along roadsides.

June-October

Virginia A. Phelps

95

Cardamine bulbosa Schreb. ex Muhl.   Spring Cress

     A cluster of white, four-petaled flowers top this 8 to 20-inch plant. The stem and basal leaves are distinctly different from the Cut-Leaved Toothwort, *Cardamine concatenata* (Michx.) O. E. Schulz. Broadly toothed leaves clasp the stem. Basal leaves are rounded with smooth edges and long stalks. Preferring cool, moist soil, Spring Cress is found in rich woods and along springs and streams throughout much of Pennsylvania.

March-June

Robert F. Bahl

PRIMULACEAE
Primrose Family

Generally members of this family may have five petals in white, yellow or pink. Leaves are simple, opposite or whorled, and are usually elongated and pointed. Some plants are variously spotted. The Evening Primrose, not part of this family, is found in Onagraceae. Fringed Loosestrife is representative of this family.

Lysimachia ciliata L.   Fringed Loosestrife

Yellow nodding flowers with rounded, fringed petals are 0.5 to 1 inch across. Undotted leaves are paired and have fringed petioles. This leafy-stemmed perennial grows 1 to 4 feet tall, and is found in wet thickets, swamps, and edges of thickets. This plant is common throughout Pennsylvania.

June-August

Phyllis T. Monk

Phyllis T. Monk

Anagallis arvensis L.

Scarlet Pimpernel
Common Pimpernel
Introduced

Five-petaled coral-pink flowers are 0.25 inch across and grow on long stalks from leaf axils. They only open in bright sunlight. Flowers are rarely white or blue. Smooth rounded leaves are paired and clasp the 4 to 12-inch stem. This native of Eurasia may be found along roadsides and in waste places across southern Pennsylvania, more commonly in the east.

June-August

Esther G. Allen

Dodecatheon meadia L
    syn. *Dodecatheon
    amethystinum* Fassett

Shooting Star

Several pink to lilac flowers at the top of the 8 to 18-inch flower stalk have three to seven swept-back lobes and a "beak" of fused yellow stamens. A basal rosette of leaves is 10 to 24 inches across, and leaves are marked with red at the base. This plant grows in open meadows, moist hillsides, and prairies, and is uncommon in Pennsylvania.

April-June

Lysimachia quadrifolia L.

Whorled Loosestrife

Four or more yellow flowers form on stalks from the upper leaf axils. Petals have a red dot and red streaks. Leaves are in whorls of four, sometimes five. The erect stems grow 1 to 3 feet tall in moist or dry uplands, thickets or open woods. This plant is common in Pennsylvania.

June-August

Robert F. Bahl

Lysimachia nummularia L.

Moneywort
Creeping Jenny
Introduced

Golden yellow flowers are 0.6 to 1 inch across and occur as pairs in leaf axils. Leaves are 0.5 to 1 inch long, rounded, opposite and short petioled. This smooth herbaceous plant has creeping stems and dark, smooth, dotted leaves. It is found in damp ground, frequently near buildings, and is common throughout Pennsylvania.

July-September

Robert F. Bahl

119

Robert F. Bahl

Lysimachia terrestris (L.)

Yellow Loosestrife
Swamp Loosestrife
Bulb-bearing Loosestrife

This smooth plant has a slender spike of five-petaled flowers. Each slender petal has red dots at the base. Leaves are paired along the 8 to 38-inch stem with slender shoots coming from the upper leaf axils. It grows in swampy areas, low ground, and wet thickets and is common throughout Pennsylvania.

June-August

Robert F. Bahl

Lysimachia thytsifolia L.

Tufted Loosestrife
Water Loosestrife

Tiny yellow flowers in tight clusters 0.5 to 2 inches across are on stalks that arise in the leaf axils of the middle stem leaves. The dotted leaves are paired and are 2 to 5 inches long. The plant grows 12 to 28 inches from a creeping rhizome, and is found in northeastern and north-western Pennsylvania.

May-July

Lysimachia vulgaris L.   Garden Loosestrife
                                                          Introduced

The yellow flowers are in a terminal cluster and also in the upper leaf axils. The five petals are smooth and the stamens are red. Leaves are in whorls on the 3-foot tall stem. The plant is softly pubescent and grows along roadsides and in swampy thickets mostly in the eastern counties of Pennsylvania.

June-September

Robert F. Bahl

Trientalis borealis Raf.   Starflower

Two to six star-shaped white flowers are on short pedicels above the whorl of slender leaves. Usually there are seven petals, an unusual characteristic. Five to nine shiny leaves 1.6 to 4 inches long cluster near the top of the stem. This perennial plant grows 3 to 8 inches high in cool, moist, rich woods and bogs throughout Pennsylvania.

May-June

Robert F. Bahl

121

HYDRANGEACEAE
Hydrangea Family

The Hydrangea Family consists of shrubs with opposite and simple leaves and white flowers. Wild Hydrangea is representative of this family.

—————

Hydrangea arborescens L.   Wild Hydrangea

A cyme of two flower types characterizes this shrub. Numerous small fertile flowers are in the center, and sterile white flowers with three or four flat petals are at the margin of the flower cluster. Leaves are opposite, ovate, 3 to 6 inches long with serrated margins. These shrubs grow 2.5 to 8.5 feet tall in woods and along streambanks throughout Pennsylvania.

June-July

Esther G. Allen

Parnassia glauca Raf.   Grass-of-Parnassus

The 0.75 to 1.5-inch wide flower has white petals heavily veined in green. Yellow-tipped stamens alternate with the petals. There is a single pair of clasping leaves on the 6 to 16-inch flower stalk. Long-petioled heart-shaped basal leaves are 0.6 to 1.8 inch wide. This smooth perennial grows 8 to 16 inches high in wet meadows and limestone bogs, and is not common in Pennsylvania.

July-October

Virginia A. Phelps

Penthorum sedoides L.

Ditch Stonecrop

Greenish flowers in branching clusters are 0.8 to 3 inches wide and top the stems. Flowers occur on the upper side of the branched stalks. Lance-shaped, sharply serrate, alternate leaves 2 to 4 inches long clasp the stem. This is an erect, smooth, perennial, growing 8 to 24 inches high, and is found in wet areas and riverbanks throughout Pennsylvania.

July-September

Robert F. Bahl

127

Saxifraga pensylvanica L.

Swamp Saxifrage

Greenish-white flowers grow in branched clusters on erect stems. Clustered basal leaves are 4 to 10 inches long. This perennial grows 1 to 4 feet tall in wet meadows, bogs, and riverbanks throughout Pennsylvania.

May-June

Robert F. Bahl

Saxifraga virginiensis Michx.

Early Saxifrage

The five-petaled white flowers have ten yellow stamens. When the first flowers open the flower stalk is 4 to 12 inches high, but later this stalk will grow up to 16 inches. Basal pubescent leaves are 1 to 3 inches long. This perennial grows 4 to 16 inches high in dry, rocky areas through-out Pennsylvania.

March-May

Virginia A. Phelps

Coronilla varia L.

Crown Vetch
Introduced

The pink or white flowers grow in dense umbels from leaf axils and are 1 to 1.5 inches across. The leaves have eleven to twenty-five oblong leaflets. This is a perennial herb with stems 1 to 3 feet long. Crown Vetch has been planted on steep hillsides along highways to prevent soil erosion and increase soil fertility. This plant often escapes to other areas and may also be found in waste places across Pennsylvania.

June-August

Walter J. Gardill

Desmodium canadense (L.) DC.

Showy Tick-trefoil
Beggar-ticks

Dense terminal racemes of purplish flowers 0.35 to 0.5-inch long grow on the numerous branches of this plant. The thin, ovate, nearly smooth three-parted leaves are 1 to 2 inches long. This perennial herb has stems that grow 2 to 8 feet long. The triangular seeds are covered with hooked bristles. This plant is found in woods, along riverbanks, and in sandy soils and is not very common in Pennsylvania.

July-August

Esther G. Allen

145

Lathyrus latifolius L.

Everlasting Pea
Introduced

The flowers of this perennial herbaceous vine may be purple, pink, or white. Flower stalks bear a raceme of four to ten large pea-like flowers, each of which is 1 inch across. Leaflets are paired and accompanied by twining tendrils at the end. Stems are trailing with flattened wings on each side. This native of Europe has been cultivated as an ornamental, and has escaped to roadsides and vacant areas and is not common in Pennsylvania.

Robert F. Bahl

June-September

Lespedeza intermedia (S. Wats.) Britt. 　　　　　　　　Bush-clover

Purple flowers are in short clusters in the upper leaf axils. Leaves are slender with long petioles, and have oval leaflets. The leaves grow densely on the stems. The erect slender stems grow 1 to 3 feet tall. This plant is found in dry upland woods, and is common throughout Pennsylvania.

July-September

Robert F. Bahl

Lotus corniculatus L.   Birdsfoot Trefoil
                                                                Introduced

Bright yellow pea-like flowers are tinged with crimson and grow in clusters of three to six. The clusters are 1 to 2 inches across. The five-parted sessile leaves are 0.25 to 0.66-inch long. This perennial herb grows in low clumps with stems 4 to 24 inches long. The seedpod resembles a bird's foot. This plant is often found growing along roadways and in waste places throughout Pennsylvania.

May-August

Virginia A. Phelps

Lupinus perennis L.

Wild Lupine

Blue, pink, or white flowers occur in loose racemes 6 to 12 inches long. Palmately divided leaves consist of seven to eleven leaflets 2 to 3 inches wide. The name "Lupine" is derived from the Latin "lupus" meaning, "wolf" because the plants were thought to weaken the soil. Wild Lupine is a perennial herb that grows 1 to 2 feet tall. It is a roadside plant of dry and sandy soils and is found mainly in central and eastern Pennsylvania.

April-July

Esther G. Allen

147

Esther G. Allen

Medicago sativa L.

Alfalfa
Introduced

Blue to violet flowers grow in clusters 0.25 to 0.5-inch long. Three-part leaves grow at the stem nodes and are 0.5 to 1 inch long. The sprawling hairy stems grow 1 to 1.5 feet. Pods of this legume are twisted spirally. Alfalfa restores nitrates to the soil and it is cultivated and used as feed for cattle. This plant often escapes cultivation and is found along roadsides in much of Pennsylvania.

May-October

Phyllis T. Monk

Melilotus alba Medic.

White Sweet Clover
Introduced

Fragrant white pea-like flowers form tapering clusters 2 to 4 inches tall at the top of freely branching stems. The three-parted leaves are 1 to 1.5 inch long. The stiff erect stems grow 2 to 5 feet tall. This plant is similar to the Yellow Sweet Clover, but blooms a week or so later. A native of Europe, this plant is common along roadsides and in rich soils.

June-October

Trifolium virginicum Small   Kate's-Mountain Clover

The yellowish-white heads of this clover are 0.5 to 1 inch wide. The leaves are three-parted with lanceolate leaflets 1.5 to 4 inches long. This hairy perennial has stems from 4 to 8 inches long, and grows on shale barrens and in neutral soils in only three south-central counties in Pennsylvania.

May-June

Phyllis T. Monk

Vicia americana Muhl. ex Willd.

Purple Vetch
Tare

A loose raceme bears two to nine purple flowers each of which is 0.6 to 0.7-inch long. Pinnate leaves have four to seven pairs of leaflets and are 0.6 to 1.2-inch long with tendrils at the end. This is a herbaceous perennial vine having smooth stems. This species closely resembles Cow or Tufted Vetch, *Vicia cracca* L. This vine is found in fields and thickets mostly in eastern Pennsylvania.

May-July

Robert F. Bahl

153

Vicia cracca L.

Cow Vetch
Tufted Vetch
Introduced

The violet-blue flowers grow on one side of the flower stalk and are in clusters 1 to 4 inches long. This herbaceous vine has hairy tendrils at the end of leaves. The leaves have 5 to 10 narrow leaflets that are covered with fine hairs. This plant is found in fields, thickets, and waste places. Cow Vetch occurs mainly in eastern Pennsylvania.

May-August

Esther G. Allen

Gaura biennis L.

Biennial Gaura

The white flowers turn pink as they fade, and are 0.3-inch wide. Long stamens and a cross-shaped stigma droop beneath the flaring four-petaled flowers. The long tubular flower blooms in clusters of two or three on long wand-like spikes. This plant grows in fields and meadows and reaches a height of 2 to 5 feet. It is widespread in the southern two-thirds of Pennsylvania.

June-October

Jay B. Brown

Ludwigia peploides (Kunth) Raven   Primrose-willow
     ssp. *glabrescens* (Kuntze) Raven
     syn. *Jussiaea repens* L. var. glabrescens Kuntze

Long-stalked flowers 1.25-inch across grow from upper leaf axils on simple or forking branches. Entire, ovate leaves are alternate, dark green and shiny, and 1.25 to 3.5 inches long. Stems are purplish. This semi-aquatic perennial creeps on wet and muddy ground, rooting at nodes. It also floats in shallow water with its submerged roots distended into bladders. Introduced into Pennsylvania, it is spreading westward from the Delaware River, with one site in Allegheny County.

June-October

Esther G. Allen

161

Esther G. Allen

Ludwegia alternifolia L.

Seedbox

One-half-inch wide yellow flowers are on short stems in the upper leaf axils. Four broad green sepals of unequal length frame four yellow petals. Leaves are lance-shaped and pointed. The seed capsule is square at the top, hence "Seedbox." The plant grows 2 to 3 feet tall in swamps and wetlands throughout Pennsylvania.

June-August

Scott J. Shriver

Oenothera fruticosa L.
  ssp. *fruticosa*

Sundrops

This yellow flower is 1 to 2 inches across, and opens wide only in full sunlight. It has a broad four-part stigma and orange stamens. The seedpods are strongly ribbed. Leaves are lance-shaped and alternate with entire margins. This plant grows to a height of 1 to 3 feet in fields and meadows across mid- and southern Pennsylvania.

June-August

CELASTRACEAE
Staff-tree Family

This is a small family consisting of shrubs and vines. Leaves are simple; dioecious flowers are inconspicuous. Fruits are often showy. Climbing Bittersweet is representative of this family.

———•••••———

Celastrus scandens L.

Climbing Bittersweet
American Bittersweet

Greenish flowers 0.1 to 0.2-inch wide are in terminal clusters. Fruits are covered with a three-part orange capsule enclosing the bright red seeds. This is a twining, rampant, woody vine, which can grow up to 50 feet long. The alternate leathery leaves are 2 to 4 inches long, oblong, pointed, and finely toothed. This plant is becoming scarce in many areas because it has been over-collected. It may be found in thickets, woods, and along riverbanks throughout Pennsylvania.

May-June

Esther G. Allen

Euonymus obovatus Nutt.   Running Strawberry-bush

Several greenish-purple flowers 0.12-inch across emerge on short stalks from leaf axils. Later, rough and warty crimson fruits develop. Leaves are ovate, 1 to 2 inches long; wider at the ends. This is a trailing shrub with four-angled or slightly winged stems 1 to 1.5 feet long. It is found in rich, dry to damp woods, thickets, and slopes in western and eastern Pennsylvania.

May-June

Virginia A. Phelps

EUPHORBIACEAE
Spurge Family

Usually members of this family have flowers without petals. Plants have a milky sap in stems and leaves. Poinsettia is a tropical member of this family. The showy "flower" consists of colored bracts with inconspicuous flowers clustered in the center. This is mostly a tropical family, and the representative in Pennsylvania is Cypress Spurge.

Euphorbia cyparissias L.

Cypress Spurge
Graveyard Weed

Tiny yellow flowers are held between a pair of yellowish to reddish bracts. The flowers and bracts are in broad terminal umbels. Leaves are numerous and needle-like. The clustered stems are 6 to 12 inches tall, contain milky sap, and spread aggressively from horizontal rhizomes. This perennial is found along roadsides, in waste places and in old cemeteries throughout Pennsylvania.

April-August

Robert F. Bahl

Euphorbia corollata L.

Flowering Spurge

A loose cluster of white flowers, each 0.25-inch across, is set on a whorl of oblong leaves at the top of the stem. Alternate stem leaves are 0.75 to 1.5 inches long. The plant has milky sap throughout. It grows 1 to 3 feet tall and is abundant in dry open woods and fields throughout Pennsylvania.

June-October

John Kuehn

169

RHAMNACEAE
Buckthorn Family

This family consists of shrubs and small trees. Leaves are usually alternate on sometimes-thorny branches. New Jersey Tea is representative of this family.

Ceanothus americanus L.   New Jersey Tea

Dense clusters of white flowers form at the end of the current year's branches. Leaves are ovate with three ribs and toothed margins. A low shrub that produces new flowering branches each year, New Jersey Tea may grow to 3 feet tall. A tea substitute was made from the leaves during the Revolutionary War. This shrub is found in dry open woods throughout Pennsylvania.

May-September

Virginia A. Phelps

ANACARDIACEAE
Sumac Family

This is a family of trees and shrubs, most of which contain a strongly poisonous, irritating sap. The small flowers are white or green and occur in a terminal panicel. Leaves are compound and leaflets are opposite. Foliage and stems in this family are usually smooth and shiny, but some species are velvety-hairy. Since this book is limited primarily to herbaceous plants, sumacs are not illustrated. Poison Ivy is representative of this family.

Toxicodendron radicans (L.) Kuntze   Poison Ivy
    syn. *Rhus radicans* L.

This trailing or high-climbing, branching, perennial woody vine or shrub is quite variable. Many aerial roots make the mature stem resemble a fuzzy rope. Alternate leaves have three oval leaflets 2 to 4 inches long. These leaves may be glossy or dull, entire or toothed, and turn brilliant orange-scarlet in the fall. Tiny 0.13-inch wide, yellowish green, five-petaled flowers in loose panicles along the stems are followed by hard, waxy, grayish-white berry-like fruits that may persist until spring. Avoid contact because all plant parts are very toxic. It is found in thickets, woods, golf courses, beaches, and waste places throughout Pennsylvania.

Phyllis T. Monk

May-July

Virginia A. Phelps

175

OXALIDACEAE
Wood-sorrel Family

Flowers have five petals and may be white, yellow or pale purple. Numerous seeds are formed in the upright pods. Leaves are three-parted and joined to the leaf stem at the heart-shaped points. These plants require acid soil, and some are tenacious weeds. Common Wood-sorrel is representative of this family.

Oxalis acetocella L. Common Wood-sorrel
 syn. *Oxalis montana* Raf.

Dainty 1-inch flowers have white petals with rose-colored veins. Basal leaves have three heart-shaped leaflets. This perennial plant grows 2 to 6 inches high in cool, damp woods mostly in the northern tier counties of Pennsylvania.

May-July

Virginia A. Phelps

BALSAMINACEAE
Touch-me-not- Family

This family consists of herbaceous plants with irregular flowers and alternate, toothed leaves. Seed capsules are elongated and will abruptly split open lengthwise casting seeds some distance from the plant. Pale Jewelweed is representative of the family.

Impatiens pallida Nutt.

Pale Jewelweed
Touch-me-not

The canary-yellow flowers are 0.7 to 1.3 inches long. Leaves are 1 to 4 inches long, thin, oval, coarsely toothed, and alternate. In both Jewelweeds, the bland watery sap from the stem has fungicidal properties effective for athlete's foot. The sap also inhibits the toxic reaction of poison ivy if applied immediately to the affected part. This plant grows in wet places, chiefly in calcareous areas, often in shade, throughout Pennsylvania.

July-September

Robert F. Bahl

Impatiens capensis Meerb.   Jewelweed
                                                        Spotted Touch-me-not

Crimson-spotted orange flowers are 0.7 to 1.3 inches long and are cornu-
copia shaped. They have two-lobed petals below, a right-angled spur, and sac-like
sepals. The leaves are oval, coarsely toothed, and alternate. A freely branching,
translucent, succulent annual, the stem may be 0.5-inch thick and up to 8 feet tall.
When water collects on the leaves, the rounded droplets shine in the sunlight like
diamonds. The bland, watery sap from the stem is said to have fungicidal properties,
and may relieve the toxic reaction to poison ivy if applied promptly. This plant
grows in wet soil, shaded woodlands, and in sub-acid swamps throughout
Pennsylvania.

                                                              June-October

Robert F. Bahl

ASCLEPIADACEAE
Milkweed Family

The name of this family describes the thick, white sap found in the stems and leaves. The clusters of flowers have five reflexed petals with a five-parted upright cup. Flowers may be purplish, pink, orange, or white, while the leaves are oval and opposite. Fruits are pods containing numerous tufted seeds. Common Milkweed is representative of this family.

Asclepias syriaca L.   Common Milkweed

The crowded flower umbels are terminal and in the upper leaf axils, forming ball-like clusters. Flowers vary from greenish to light purple, with a strong fragrance that attracts bees. The seedpods are downy and covered with warty projections. Common Milkweed grows up to 5 feet tall. Leaves are coarse, oblong, and 4 to 6 inches long. The leaf veins are nearly perpendicular to the midrib. During wartime the seed tufts were gathered as a substitute for kapok used in life preservers. The plant serves as a host to the larval stage of the Monarch butterfly that makes its cocoon on the underside of a leaf. These plants are found throughout Pennsylvania in fields, roadsides, and waste places.

June-August

Esther G. Allen

Asclepias incarnata L. ssp. *incarnata*   Swamp Milkweed

Swamp Milkweed grows up to 5 feet high, usually branching near the top into many flat-topped umbels of rose-purple flowers. The tapered opposite leaves may be smooth or hairy in our range. The seedpods are smooth and narrow. This species requires more moisture than most of the other milkweeds and is found in wet ditches, meadows, and shorelines throughout Pennsylvania, more frequently in the northern counties.

June-August

Esther G. Allen

Scott J. Shriver

Asclepias quadrifolia Jacq.

Four-leaved Milkweed

There are usually two loose clusters of pink-tipped white flowers, which are fragrant. The plant has a slender stem 12 to 30 inches high with upper and lower leaves in pairs, the middle ones usually in whorls of four. This plant is found across Pennsylvania in dry woods.

May-July

200

Solanum nigrum L.

Common Nightshade
Black Nightshade
Introduced

     Similar to the preceding species, the flowers are whitish and the berries are dull black. It has a coarser stem and the leaves are more triangular and lack the basal lobes. A European species, this plant is poisonous, and grows in waste or cultivated areas throughout Pennsylvania.

May-October

Robert F. Bahl

CONVOLVULARIACEAE
Morning Glory Family

Members of this family have twining, vine-like stems and flaring bell-shaped flowers. Five petals are united in a spreading corolla, that may be white, pink, or blue. Leaves are triangular to heart-shaped, and they are occasionally three-lobed. The common Morning Glory is representative of this family.

Ipomoea purpurea (L.) Roth

Morning Glory
Introduced

The trumpet-shaped flowers have fused petals and are in clusters of one to five in the leaf axils. The 2 to 3-inch flowers are white, pink, purple, bluish, or even variegated. Broad leaves are heart to oval-shaped and 2 to 5 inches long. This downy, high-climbing annual vine may reach 10 feet in length. It was introduced from tropical America and, having escaped cultivation, now grows along roadsides, field edges, and fence rows, found mainly in southeastern Pennsylvania with a few other locations in the state.

July-October

Esther G. Allen

206

LAMIACEAE
Mint Family

Formerly called "Labiatae," the Mint Family members usually have square stems and aromatic glands. Leaves are opposite and usually toothed. Flowers have upper and lower "lips," and may be white, yellow, pink, or lavender. Gill-over- the-Ground is representative of this family.

Glechoma hederacea L.

Gill-Over-the-Ground
Ground Ivy
Introduced

Violet to blue flowers grow 0.3 to 0.5-inch long from the upper leaf axils. The lower lip has purple spots. Leaves are rounded, 1 to 2 inches long, and bluntly toothed. The lower stem creeps along the ground and sends up 3 to 5-inch square stems. Introduced from Europe, this plant grows along roadsides, lawns, and shady places throughout Pennsylvania.

April- July

Virginia A. Phelps

223

Ajuga reptans L.

Bugle Weed
Introduced
Escape

Bright blue flowers 0.5-inch long grow among numerous upper stem leaves. Smooth basal leaves are copper or purplish in color and clasp the square hairy stem. The 6 to 15 inch high plant grows from a creeping runner, and is found in fields and along road-sides. This plant is not common in Pennsylvania.

Robert F. Bahl

May-July

Blephilia ciliata (L.) Benth.

Downy Wood-mint

Several terminal whorls of pale purple or white flowers are 0.5 to 1 inch across. Leaves are sessile or short-stalked, some-what toothed, and are 1 to 2 inches long. This hairy perennial grows 1 to 2 feet high in dry woods and open fields mostly in western Pennsylvania.

June-August

Esther G. Allen

Collinsonia canadensis L.

Horse Balm
Richweed
Stoneroot

    Pale yellow flowers are 0.5 inch long in loose, branching panicles. They have a fringed lower lip and are lemon scented. Opposite leaves are broadly ovate, toothed, and 6 to 10 inches long. This erect, square-stemmed plant grows in damp, rich woods throughout Pennsylvania.

July- September

Virginia A. Phelps

Cunila origanoides (L.) Britt.

Stone Mint
American Dittany
Horsemint

    Clusters of 0.5-inch purple-spotted pink flowers grow terminally and in leaf axils. Leaves are 0.5 to 1.5 inches long and are paired along the square stems. They are dotted with many clear spots. This perennial is woody at the base and grows 8 to 20 inches high in woods, clearings, dry hills and thickets, mostly in eastern Pennsylvania.

July-October

Esther G. Allen

225

Hedeoma pulegioides (L.) Pers.

American Pennyroyal

Clumps of bluish tubular flowers are held in a prominent toothed calyx in the leaf axils. Flower stalks are multi-branched. Leaves are narrow and deeply veined, paired along the hairy stems. This aromatic annual grows 6 to 18 inches tall in dry soil throughout Pennsylvania.

July-September

Phyllis T. Monk

Lamium amplexicaule L.

Henbit
Introduced

A whorl of purplish, erect flowers 0.5 to 0.75-inch long grow in the upper leaf axils. Upper stem leaves clasp around the square stem and lower stem leaves have petioles. Leaves are 0.5 to 1.5 inches long, and are rounded with scalloped edges. This annual grows 6 to 18 inches high along roadsides and in waste places throughout the lower one-third of Pennsylvania.

March-November

Robert F. Bahl

Lamium purpureum L.

Purple Dead Nettle
Red Henbit
Introduced

Purple to reddish flowers 0.5-inch long nestle closely in the upper leaves. The lower lip of the flower is reduced to short teeth. The overlapping heart-shaped leaves are hairy and the uppermost are purplish. "Dead Nettle' refers to the non-irritating nature of the plant. Often growing in masses, this plant may be found along roadsides and in waste places in southern counties of Pennsylvania.

April-October

Phyllis T. Monk

Leonurus cardiaca L.

Motherwort
Introduced

Pink, purple or white flowers 0.3 to 0.5-inch grow in the leaf axils of the upper stem. The upper lip of the flower is bearded. Leaves are paired and have long petioles. Upper leaves are toothed and lower leaves have three or five toothed lobes. This perennial grows 2 to 4 feet tall on stout square stems. It grows along roadsides and waste areas throughout Pennsylvania.

June-August

Robert F. Bahl

Monarda clinopodia L.

Basil Balm

White to yellowish dark-spotted flowers 1 to 1.6 inches long lie among greenish bracts in a dense head. Opposite leaves are 2 to 4 inches long and are lanceolate, hairy, and toothed. This perennial plant grows up to 39 inches tall in rich woods and thickets throughout Pennsylvania.

June-July

Robert F. Bahl

Monarda didyma L.

Oswego Tea
Bee Balm

Bright scarlet tubular flowers are 1.5 to 2 inches long in dense heads. Opposite leaves are 3 to 6 inches long. This hairy perennial has square stems and grows 2 to 3 feet tall in wet areas, thickets, and along streambanks throughout Pennsylvania.

Another similar species is Purple Bergamot *Monarda media* Willd., (Not illustrated), has red-purple flowers. Similar to the above, it is less common in Pennsylvania.

June-September

Esther G. Allen

Conopholis americana (L.) Wallr.   Squawroot

    Yellowish tubular flowers are 0.5 inch long, and have a hooded upper lip and a three-parted lower one. The flowers protrude from yellowish-brown scales, which cover a thick, fleshy spike 2 to 10 inches high. This parasitic native plant lacks chlorophyll and resembles the cone of a white pine. It forms clusters of plants on roots of deciduous trees, especially oaks. This plant is found in woods, usually under oaks scattered throughout the southern tier counties of Pennsylvania.

May-June

Virginia A. Phelps

Epifagus virginiana (L.) Bart.

Beech-drops

    Two kinds of whitish flowers are on branched stems. Upper, sterile ones are 0.5 inch long, tubular, and curved with four teeth. Lower flowers never open, but produce seed by self-pollination. Pale brownish-yellowish stems with small scattered scales grow 6 to 18 inches high. The roots of Beech-drops penetrate the underground tissue of Beech trees. This parasitic plant may be found in woods throughout Pennsylvania.

August-October

Scott J. Shriver

255

ACANTHACEAE
Acanthus Family

Members of this family have simple opposite leaves and tubular flowers. Smooth Ruellia is representative of this family.

Ruellia strepens L.

Smooth Ruellia
Wet Petunia

One or several pale bluish to purplish 1.5 to 2 inch long trumpet-shaped flowers grow in the axils of leaves. Three to 5 inch long alternate leaves taper at the base and tip. This is an erect perennial with a smooth to slightly downy, sometimes branching, four-sided stem that is 1 to 4 feet high. In addition, this plant may have cleistogamous flowers. Located in dry woods, this plant is rare in Pennsylvania.

May-July

Esther G. Allen

Justicia americana (L.) Vahl   Water-willow

    Clusters of white 1.5-inch long flowers with purplish markings are on long stalks in leaf axils. The upper lip is notched and arched; the lower is three-lobed and recurved. Long, willow-like leaves are 3 to 8 inches long, entire and opposite. This is a strong herbaceous, perennial, emergent water plant with thick rhizomes and stems up to 3.5 feet. Water-willow forms large colonies in swamps and along the edges of streams, ponds, and lakes. Because of its leaf shape, the plant is frequently assumed to be a small willow, however the two are not related. This plant grows in shallow water and along wet shores scattered throughout Pennsylvania.

June-October

Virginia A. Phelps

BIGNONIACEAE
Catalpa Family

This family is made up of trees and woody vines that are mostly tropical. The Trumpet Creeper and Catalpa tree are common in southern Pennsylvania. Flowers are tubular and showy. They may be white, pinkish or bright red. Trumpet Creeper is representative of this family.

Campsis radicans (L.) Seem.   Trumpet Creeper

Very showy, bright orange to scarlet trumpet-shaped flowers 2.5 to 3 inches long are in clusters. Leaves are pinnately compound with seven to eleven ovate, pointed and toothed leaflets, 2.5 to 3 inches long. This native woody perennial grows up to 50 feet, and has aerial rootlets. It is frequently cultivated for its flowers and because it attracts hummingbirds, but it may become weedy. This plant is found in low woods, thickets, and streambanks in the southern tier counties.

July-September

Virginia A. Phelps

LENTIBULARIACEAE
Bladderwort Family

Members of this family are insectivorous and grow in water or damp soil. Tiny air-filled bladders located along the submerged stems and leaves are adapted to capture swimming insects. Flowers are small and have two flaring lips. Common Bladderwort is representative of this family.

———•·••·•———

Utricularia macrorhiza Le Conte   Common Bladderwort
   syn. *Utricularia vulgaris* L.

Bright yellow flowers and larger bladders distinguish this from the other species of Bladderworts. The illustration shows the erect flower stalk emerging from the water. The finely divided leaves may grow in wet soil as well as submerged in water. It may be found in a few northeastern counties of Pennsylvania.

May-September

Robert F. Bahl

Utricularia cornuta Michx.   Horned Bladderwort

The yellow flower is   trumpet-shaped, and there are usually 1 to 3 flowers on an erect stem.   The underwater stem has tiny bladders. This plant is able to grow in wet soil as well as submerged in water, and is found in a few counties of northeastern Pennsylvania.

June-September

Robert F. Bahl

Utricularia purpurea Walt.   Purple Bladderwort

The 0.4 to 0.6-inch flower is purple or deep pink, and consists of a spur and three-petal lobes.   The stem is mostly submerged with whorls of long-stalked leaves, some of which have ovoid bladders at the tips. When the plant is in flower the bladders float at the surface. The bladders are traps adapted for capturing aquatic insects. This plant grows in slow streams, shallow ponds and wet places in a few Delaware River counties.

June-September

Robert F. Bahl

CAPRIFOLIACEAE
Honeysuckle Family

Flowers are tubular and may be white, yellow, or red to pink. Leaves may vary from simple, small and rounded, to compound and coarsely toothed. These leaves grow opposite each other along the stem. Woody vines and shrubs make up this family, and Twinflower is a representative.

Phyllis T. Monk

Linnaea borealis L. var. *americana* (Forbes) Rehd.

Twinflower

Two pink bell-shaped flowers top the 3 to 5-inch flower stalk. Leaves are 0.25 to 0.7 inch long and evergreen. This woody creeping plant grows in cool woods, and bogs, and is rare in Pennsylvania. Carolus Linnaeus, father of systemized botany, named this plant for himself. It was his favorite and he is always pictured holding one.

June-August

Virginia A. Phelps

269

Phyllis T. Monk

Lonicera japonica Thunb.
var. *japonica*

Japanese Honeysuckle
Introduced

White tubular very fragrant flowers are 1 inch long, and have protruding stamens. As they age they turn yellow. The fruit is a black berry. Leaves are 1 inch long and are opposite each other along the stem. This herbaceous woody shrub was used in the past for covering banks of roadcuts. Difficult to eradicate, this plant grows in thickets, edges of woods, fencerows and along roadsides. It is found mostly in south-central and southeastern Pennsylvania.

April-July

Esther G. Allen

Lonicera sempervirens L.

Trumpet Honeysuckle
Introduced

Narrow tubular flowers are red outside and yellow inside, 1 to 1.5 inches long, and grow in whorls at the ends of branches. The leaves below the flowers are joined around the stem. Lower leaves are oblong-pointed, whitish below, and clasp the stem. This is a climbing shrub that grows in fields and thickets mostly in southeastern Pennsylvania.

April-September

270

Arctium minus (Hill) Bernh.

Common Burdock
Introduced

In the first year this plant develops a long root and a whorl of large leaves that resemble rhubarb. The second year it produces a tall stalk with purplish flower heads surrounded by bristly bracts that become burs with curved hooks. Flower heads are 0.5 inch wide. One can fashion baskets or chains from the ripened burs. The root is sometimes sold in the markets as "Wild Gobo." This biennial plant grows from 1 to 5 feet tall along roadsides and in waste ground throughout Pennsylvania.

Jay B. Brown

July-October

Arctium tomentosum P. Mill.

Wooly Burdock
Introduced

Similar to the Great Burdock, *Arctium lappa* L., this species has numerous fine hairs on the hooked bracts on the base of the flower head. The flower heads are usually smaller, from 0.75 to 1-inch in diameter, and the leaf stalks are hollow. This plant grows 4 to 9 feet tall in waste places and is not very common in Pennsylvania.

July-September

Phyllis T. Monk
279

Esther G. Allen

Aster lateriflorus (L.) Britt.

Calico Aster

This aster gets its name "calico" because the 0.5-inch heads have disk flowers that are first yellow, then turn reddish-purple. Flowers on one plant may include both colors at the same time. Its tiny flower heads have nine to fifteen ray flowers. This perennial grows from 1 to 5 feet tall in dry open areas throughout Pennsylvania.

August-October

Jay B. Brown

Aster linariifolius L.

Stiff Aster

The stiff leafy stalk holds several flower heads with blue ray flowers and a yellow center disk. Flower heads are 1 inch wide and the plant may grow from 8 to 18 inches tall. Stiff Aster grows in dry sandy or rocky soil occurring mostly in the eastern part of Pennsylvania.

August-October

Aster novae-angliae L.

New England Aster

Flower color ranges from bright lavender to purplish-blue, with magenta probably the most common. Flower heads are 1 to 2 inches across. Tightly crowded leaves clasp the stem. This is the showiest native wild aster, and it is frequently lifted from the wild and planted in gardens. It grows from 3 to 7 feet tall and may be found in fields, damp meadows, and along shores throughout Pennsylvania.

August-October

Esther G. Allen

Aster pilosus Willd. var. *pilosus*

Heath Aster

The white flowers of this native perennial are 0.5 to 1 inch across and are usually quite numerous. "Pilosus," meaning "with long hairs," is a misnomer, because frequently the stems and leaves are smooth. The branched stems have many short, narrow leaves, while those on the flower stalks are so small they are called "bracta." This plant grows 1 to 5 feet tall throughout Pennsylvania.

August-October

Virginia A. Phelps

Esther G. Allen

Aster prenanthoides Muhl. ex Willd.

Crooked-stem Aster
Zig-zag Aster

This native perennial can be recognized from the smooth zigzag stem and clasping leaves that are toothed at the far ends, but toothless toward the stem. Pale violet flower heads are 1 to 1.6 inches wide. It grows 1 to 3 feet tall along wood edges, banks, and wet thickets throughout Pennsylvania.

August-October

Esther G. Allen

Aster puniceus L. ssp. *firmus* (Nees) A.G. Jones

Purple-stemmed Aster

Pale violet flower heads are 1 to 1.6 inches wide. "Puniceus" means "Phoenician purple," describing the color of the bristly stem of this native perennial. The plant reaches a height of 2 to 8 feet while growing in swamps and wet thickets throughout Pennsylvania.

August-November

Aster umbellatus P. Mill   Flat-topped White Aster

This native perennial has few-rayed flowers that form a flat-topped cluster that is almost 12 inches across. The yellow disks turn purple as they age. There may be as many as two to fifteen ray flowers. Flower heads are 0.5 to 0.8 inches across; height may be 1 to 7 feet. This is a very conspicuous aster of wet places, occurring throughout Pennsylvania.

August-September

Esther G. Allen

Bellis perennis L.

English Daisy
Introduced

Rosy-tipped ray flowers surround the yellow disk flowers in the 0.5 to 1-inch flower head. The word "daisy" comes from the Anglo-Saxon term, "daeges eye" (day's eye), which refers to the habit of the flower closing at night and opening during the day. The plant grows 1.2 to 7 inches high, often in lawns, and has become established in several areas in Pennsylvania.

April-November

Esther G. Allen

283

Bidens cernua L.   Nodding Bur-marigold
                                                              Stick-tight

    The heads, which may or may not have ray flowers, are up to 2 inches across. Leaves are toothed and elongated. "Bidens" means "two teeth," referring to the two hooks on the seeds. These hooks catch on passing fur or clothing, giving the plant its other name, "Stick–tights." This plant is native to both the New and the Old World. It may grow from 1 to 3 feet tall in wet soil throughout Pennsylvania.

July-October

Jay B. Brown

Robert F. Bahl

Bidens frondosa L.

Beggar-ticks

    Five to nine narrow leaf-like bracts forming an involucre surround flower heads, which usually lack ray flowers. This troublesome weed is an annual, native to North America. The plant grows from 2 to 3 feet tall in wet or dry soil throughout Pennsylvania.

July-October

Cacalia atriplicifolia L.   Pale Indian-plantain

    Whitish flowers are in flat-topped clusters. Each flower head is about 0.5-inch across. Basal leaves are broadly toothed or lobed and irregular. Stem leaves are smaller and wedge-shaped. Stems are smooth with a whitish bloom and grow 3 to 6 feet tall. This native perennial is common in Pennsylvania.

July-September

Mary Lou Brown

Phyllis T. Monk

Carduus nutans L.

Nodding Thistle
Introduced

This plant is a biennial with drooping flower heads. Numerous pink to red tubular flowers are held in an involucre of purplish bracts. Leaves are very spiny with many lobes and teeth. Two to 9-foot stems have spiny ridges. This species grows in fields and waste places, and is designated as a weed, and is more common in southeast Pennsylvania.

June-October

Richard McDermot

Centaurea cyanus L.

Bachelor's Button
Introduced

Flowers are 1.5 to 2 inches across and are usually blue, but may be pink or white. The plant grows 1 to 2.5 feet tall. The name Bachelor's Button comes from the button-like flower head that is round and hard. In bygone days in England, young maidens would wear the flower as a sign that they were unmarried and looking for an available bachelor. This annual is a European import that has escaped cultivation and is scattered in eastern Pennsylvania.

July-September

Robert F. Bahl

Cirsium muticum Michx.

Swamp Thistle

Flower heads, 1 inch broad and 1 inch high, are usually clustered at the tip of the stem. Leaves are deeply cut without sharp spines. In this native species, the flowering stem is hollow and spineless, and reaches a height of 10 feet. This biennial grows in swamps, wet woods, and thickets throughout Pennsylvania.

July-September

Esther G. Allen

Cirsium pumilum (Nutt.) Spreng.

Pasture Thistle

The flower heads are 2 to 3 inches across with a spreading crown of purple or white flowers in a prickly involucre. The stem is covered with fine hairs. The plant grows 1 to 3 feet tall. Pasture Thistle is our largest flowered thistle, and is very fragrant. This biennial grows in dry soil and in pastures throughout Pennsylvania.

June-September

Esther G. Allen

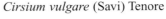

Cirsium vulgare (Savi) Tenore

Bull Thistle
Introduced

Flower heads are 1.5 to 2 inches across. This is the spiniest of the thistles and is often pictured with a goldfinch. This bird is particularly fond of the seeds, and delays nest building until late summer, when it gathers large amounts of thistle down for nest lining. A native of Eurasia, Bull Thistle is a biennial that grows a rosette of basal leaves the first year and a 2 to 6-foot tall flowering stalk the next year. Bull Thistle is a common roadside plant across Pennsylvania.

Robert F. Bahl   June-September

Conyza canadensis (L.) Cronq.
var. *canadensis*

Horseweed

A multitude of whitish flowers make up a long and many-branched flower head. Individual flowers have extended pappal bristles and twenty-five to forty shorter white or pinkish ray flowers emerging from an elongated involucre. Stem leaves are slightly downy, from 2 to 3.5 inches long. Basal leaves are broader and toothed, but have usually withered on flowering plants. This annual plant grows 1 to 5 feet tall in old fields and waste places across Pennsylvania.

Phyllis T. Monk   August-October

Coreopsis lanceolata L.

Lance-leaved Coreopsis
Tickseed
Introduced

Virginia A. Phelps

The yellow ray flowers have four points at the tips and the flower heads are 2 to 6 inches across. Leaves are narrow and elongated. Coreopsis comes from two Greek words; *"koris"* meaning "bedbug" and *"opsis"* meaning, "looks like." The tiny fruits resemble small bugs or ticks. This plant grows from 1 to 3 feet tall. This perennial is native to the Midwest, but has escaped from cultivation eastward, growing in poor soils, roadsides, and dry, sandy places mostly in eastern Pennsylvania.

May-August

Erigeron annuus (L.) Pers.

Daisy Fleabane

The flower head is 0.5 wide with 50 to 100 white ray flowers surrounding the yellow disk. It grows from 1 to 5 feet tall and is a common weed of open fields. The word "bane," comes from the Anglo-Saxon *"bana,"* which means "destroyer." Dried fleabane plants were thought to be an insect repellant. Daisy Fleabane is a native annual that is common throughout Pennsylvania.

May-October

Robert F. Bahl

Erigeron philadelphicus L.

Philadelphia Fleabane
Common Fleabane

Flowers vary from white to pink to rose-purple. The flower head is 0.5 to 1 inch across. Narrow toothed leaves clasp the stem. This plant bears the name of Pennsylvania's largest city and is a native perennial. It grows from 6 inches to 3 feet tall and is common in open woods and fields throughout Pennsylvania.

April-August

Esther G. Allen

Eupatorium coelestinum L.

Mistflower

Fuzzy bluish-violet flower heads resemble the cultivated *Ageratum* sp., which is native to North America. Leaves have blunt teeth and are opposite on 1 to 3-foot tall stems. This flower grows in moist woods and thickets in the southern tier counties of Pennsylvania.

August-October

Jay B. Brown

Hieracium venosum L.   Rattlesnake-weed

    The golden yellow flower heads are 0.5 to 0.75-inch across, and there are usually several at the tips of the branched stem. This is the only common Rattlesnake Weed that has prominent red veins in the 1 to 5-inch oblanceolate basal leaves. The stem is usually smooth with few if any leaves, and the plant grows 1 to 2.5 feet tall. This perennial is found in upland woods and edges of woods throughout most of Pennsylvania.

May-October

Robert F. Bahl

Inula helenium L.   Elecampane
Introduced

    The flowers are 2 to 4 inches across and have numerous narrow ray flowers. Broadly pointed and finely toothed leaves are wooly beneath and clasp the stout stem. Over 2000 years ago, Hippocrates prescribed the root of Elecampane for lung ailments. Of Eurasian origin, the colonists brought this plant to North America. This plant grows 2 to 6 feet tall and has occasionally escaped to roadsides and fields, now scattered throughout Pennsylvania.

July-September

Esther G. Allen   303

Krigia biflora (Walt.) S.F. Blake

Two-flowered Cynthia
Dwarf Dandelion

The yellow-orange flower heads consist entirely of ray flowers that are 1 to 1.5 inches across. Thin bracts are reflexed with age. Leaves are basal except for a single clasping leaf where the upper stem forks into two flower stalks. This plant grows 1 to 2.5 feet tall in wet meadows and woods primarily in the eastern and western counties of Pennsylvania.

May-August

Robert F. Bahl

Latuca canadensis L. var. *canadensis*

Wild Lettuce

Pale yellow flower heads are 0.2 to 0.25-inch across and are longer than they are wide. The upper stem has many branches with numerous flowers. Leaves vary from 4 to 14 inches long and may be deeply lobed to arrow-shaped. Leaves clasp the smooth stem that grows from 3 to 10 feet tall. This plant is common along roadsides, fields and in woods throughout Pennsylvania.

July-September

Robert F. Bahl

Rose-purple, sometimes white, flower heads cover a 1 to 2-foot spike that is 1.5 to 2 inches across. Flower heads at the top of the spike open first. Stems are stiff and erect from 1 to 5 feet tall. Growing in moist meadows in southeastern Pennsylvania, this plant has become established at Jennings' Blazing Star Prairie. Otto E. Jennings, who was secretary and later president of the Botanical Society of Western Pennsylvania, has this remnant prairie named in his honor.

July-September

Esther G. Allen

Phyllis T. Monk

Marshallia grandiflora Beadle & F.E. Boyton

Barbara's Buttons

The pale purple-pink flower head arises from a tapering receptacle at the top of a 1 to 2 foot stem. Leaves are mostly basal, elongated and toothless. This perennial grows on flood-scoured rock shelves and shores. In Pennsylvania this plant reaches its northern limit at Ohiopyle State Park in Fayette County. It is listed under the Pennsylvania Wild Plant Conservation Act and the Federal Endangered Species Act.

June-July

Robert F. Bahl

Matricaria matricarioides (Less.) Porter

Pineapple-weed
Introduced

Conical rayless flowers are 0.25 to 0.5-inch across. Leaves are highly branched and divided. This plant may grow 6 to 8 inches tall. When bruised it has the odor of pineapple. The rayless yellow heads have a faint visual resemblance to little pineapples. Pineapple-weed, an annual, is indigenous to the Pacific states, but has become naturalized, not only in eastern North America, but in Europe as well. It may be found along roadsides and in waste places throughout Pennsylvania except the southwest.

June-October

Petasites hybridus (L.) Gaertn, Mey. & Scherb.

Sweet Coltsfoot
Butterbur
Introduced

Stout, hollow stems support compact spikes of rayless lilac-pink flowers. This plant grows 6 to 12 inches tall. "Petasites" in Greek means a "broad-rimmed hat," referring to the huge leaves that may be 2 feet across. A perennial from Europe and northern Asia, this plant grows in waste ground in southeastern Pennsylvania.

April-May

Esther G. Allen

Prenanthes altissima L.

Rattlesnake-root
Tall White Lettuce

The nodding, greenish-white flowers are 0.5-inch long and have a protruding style and anthers. Leaves are thin, glabrous above and hirsute beneath. Stem leaves are shallowly lobed or toothed, and basal leaves vary considerably from triangular to heart-shaped with long petioles. The stout stem is smooth in the upper part and hirsute near the base, and contains a milky sap. This plant grows 0.5 to 7 feet tall in woodlands throughout Pennsylvania.

August-September

Robert F. Bahl

Esther G. Allen

Ratibida pinnata (Vent.) Barnh.

Gray-headed Coneflower

Flower rays are 1 to 2.5 inches long. Flowers give off an anise scent when bruised. The cone-shaped disk is 1 inch tall. This native perennial resembles a Black-eyed Susan with strongly reflexed petals. This plant grows from 1.5 to 5 feet tall. Mostly a Midwestern species of dry woods and prairies, there are very few stations in Pennsylvania. This plant is listed in the Pennsylvania Wild Plant Conservation Act.

June-September

Esther G. Allen

Rudbeckia hirta L. var. *hirta*

Black-eyed Susan

From ten to twenty yellow ray flowers surround the dark brown disk. The earliest flowers appear in June, and the plants continue to flower until fall. This plant is a biennial, forming a leafy rosette in the first year. Growing 1 to 3 feet tall, it may be found in dry fields, open woods, waste places and gardens through-out Pennsylvania.

June-October

Solidago canadensis L. var.
   scabra Torr. & A. Gray

Tall Goldenrod

This plant has a plume-like spire of branched flower stalks at the top. Individual flower heads are 0.25-inch across with numerous yellow ray flowers. The stem is grayish and rough. Leaves closely spaced along the stem are rough textured, and are 0.25 to 5 inches long with fine teeth along the margins. This is one of the tallest Goldenrods growing from 2 to 7 feet high. Tall Goldenrod is a native plant that occurs in dry open areas and is common across Pennsylvania.

August-November

Virginia A. Phelps

Solidago juncea Ait.

Early Goldenrod

This plant is a native perennial with flowers 0.3-inch across in a plume-like head. The upper stem leaves are slender and toothless with several smaller leaves inserted at the base. Basal leaves are pointed and sharply toothed. This plant grows 1.5 to 4 feet tall in dry soil on roadsides, fields, and open woods throughout Pennsylvania.

July- September

Esther G. Allen

313

Solidago rugosa Ait. var. *rugosa*

Rough-stemmed Goldenrod

The light yellow heads of this Goldenrod are 2 to 4 inches across. Each head has eight to eleven ray flowers and three to eight disk flowers. Stem leaves are numerous and crowded, each with prominent veins. The stems are 1 to 7 feet tall, and are covered with long, soft hairs. These plants are located throughout Pennsylvania.

Robert F. Bahl   July-November

Solidago sempervirens L.

Seaside Goldenrod

The yellow flower heads are 0.25 to 0.5 inch across, and have twelve to seventeen ray flowers and seventeen to twenty-two disk flowers. Basal leaves are thick and fleshy, entire, and vary from 4 to 16 inches long. Stem leaves are smaller and numerous. The 2 to 7-foot stems arise from a basal caudex and may be smooth or downy. These plants are located in salt marshes and sea beaches in the southeastern counties of Pennsylvania.

August-December

S. G. Shetler

Veronronia gigantea (Walt.) Trel.
var. *gigantea*

Tall Ironweed

Very similar to New York Ironweed, *Vernonia novebora-censis* (L.) Michx., the flower heads are smaller and the spreading cyme is broader. Stems grow up to 10 feet tall. Both Ironweeds hybridize, and intermediate forms may be found. This form is a native perennial, growing in the damp rich soil of bottomlands, meadows and clearings and is found throughout Pennsylvania.

August-October

Jay B. Brown

Vernonia noveboracensis (L.) Michx.

New York Ironweed

A cyme of purple flower heads spreads 3 to 4 inches across. Individual flower heads are 0.5-inch. Linear leaves with short petioles are alternately arranged along the 3 to 6 foot tall stems. The name describes the extremely tough stems. It is a native perennial that grows in moist soil in thickets, ditches and along streambanks throughout Pennsylvania.

August-October

Phyllis T. Monk

Liliopsida
Monocots

The seeds of these flowering plants have a single cotyledon. Other characteristics that apply to nearly every member of this group are; flower parts are usually in multiples of three, leaf veins are parallel to one another. They have a diffuse root system, and they have a simple vascular system. This tissue is scattered in the stem, and there is no secondary support tissue. The latter characteristic limits their size. Water, minerals, and soluble plant products are carried in the vascular tissue in both the Magnoliopsida and the Liliopsida. This group is commercially important since most of the grains and cultivated ornamentals are members. Grasses are the most numerous and are the best example of Liliopsida.

Large-flowered Trillium   Mary Joy Haywood

Painted Trillium   Phyllis T. Monk

BUTOMACEAE
Flowering Rush Family

These plants have showy umbels of pink flowers and narrow leaves that arise from a fleshy rootstock. They grow in slow-moving water or muddy shores. Flowering Rush is representative of the family.

———◆•◆•◆———

Butomus umbellatus L.

Flowering Rush
Introduced

The 3.5-foot flower stalk has an umbel of numerous rose-pink flowers. Each flower is 1 inch across and has three petals and three sepals that surround several red anthers. The sword-shaped leaves, triangular in cross-section, are erect and over 3 feet tall. Introduced from Eurasia to near Montreal, this plant has spread south and west along waterways and is found along lakeshores in northwest Pennsylvania.

June-September

Virginia A. Phelps

ALISMATACEAE
Water-Plantain Family

These are herbaceous plants that grow in water or wet places. Leaves are long and broad or arrow-shaped. Flowers are in threes with white petals; fruits are achenes. Northern Water Plantain is representative of this family.

Alisma plantago-aquatica L.   Northern Water Plantain
   var. *parviflorum* (Pursh) Torr.
   syn. *A. subcordatum* Raf.

Tiny white to pinkish flower heads with three green sepals and three larger petals are on widely branching clusters. Leaves are ovate on long stalks. The plant grows from 1 to 3 feet tall in mud, swampy areas, and shallow water throughout Pennsylvania. Northern Water Plantain is listed in the Pennsylvania Wild Plant Conservation Act.

June-September

Virginia A. Phelps

323

Sagittaria latifolia Willd. var. *latifolia*   Arrowhead

   Flowers consist of three white petals surrounding a cluster of yellow stamens. The flowers occur in threes along the upper end of an unbranched stalk. The three-pointed leaves vary greatly in width. The plant grows from 3 to 5 feet tall in shallow water and is common throughout Pennsylvania.

July-August

Emily Johnson

Peltandra virginica (L.) Schott & Endl.   Arrow Arum
                                                              Tuckahoe

    The green, pointed spathe encloses a whitish spadix and is 6 to 16 inches
long. Leaves are elongated and three-pointed. Berries form near the base of the
spadix. The plant grows from 1 to 1.5 feet tall in shallow water or bogs in the
western and eastern counties of Pennsylvania.

                                                              May-July

Virginia A. Phelps

Emily Johnson

Symplocarpus foetidus (L.)
Salisb. ex Nutt.

Skunk Cabbage

The hooded spathe appears, sometimes through the snow, long before the leaves emerge from the ground. The thick fleshy spathe is 3 to 6 inches high with green and purple spots or streaks. Inside, the fat fleshy spadix has a symmetrical mosaic pattern of flowers. Later, groups of large basal ovate leaves unfold from 1 to 5 feet long. When bruised they have a disagreeable odor. This plant is found in swamps and wet places throughout Pennsylvania.

February-April

Mary Joy Haywood

COMMELINACEAE
Spiderwort Family

The Spiderwort Family consists of herbaceous plants that have narrow, parallel-veined leaves along the jointed stem. Clustered flowers at the tip of stems open one or two at a time from an enclosing sheath. Flowers are often blue and may be regular or irregular in form. Flower parts are in threes. Common Spiderwort is an example of this family.

————

Tradescantia virginiana L.

Common Spiderwort
Trinity

Clusters of three-petaled flowers and several fuzzy buds grow from the top of narrow stalks. The leaves are long and narrow, from 8 inches to 3 feet tall, with tufts of hairs where they join the stem. The blue-purple flowers are about 1 inch across and the stem grows between 6 inches to 3 feet in height. It has been cultivated as a garden plant but has escaped to roadsides, edges of woods and in meadows, in some of the southern tier counties of Pennsylvania.

April-July

Esther G. Allen

331

Commelina communis L. var. *communis*   Asiatic Dayflower
                                                          Introduced

   Growing from a mass of tapering leaves, these bright blue flowers have two large blue upper petals and an inconspicuous tiny white petal beneath. The leaves are 3 to 5 inches long and the flowers are about 0.5 to 0.7-inch wide. The common name for this annual plant indicates its Asian origin and the habit of a single day's bloom for each flower. It is similar to a less common species, Virginia Dayflower, *Commelina virginica* L., (Not illustrated), the three petals of which are blue. Asiatic Dayflower is found in moist soil, often along roadsides throughout Pennsylvania.

                                                          July-October

Virginia A. Phelps

SPARGANIACEAE
Bur-reed Family

These aquatic plants have long slender leaves along the erect stem.   Male and female flowers are separate but on the same flower stalk. Lesser Bur-reed is representative of this family.

———◆•◆◆•◆———

Sparganium americanum Nutt.

Lesser Bur-reed

Rounded heads of staminate flowers are smaller and grow directly on the stem above the 0.75 to 1-inch pistillate flower heads. Leaves are long and narrow on stems that grow up to 3 feet tall. This perennial is widely distributed along muddy shores and in shallow water throughout Pennsylvania.

May-August

Esther G. Allen

TYPHACEAE
Cattail Family

These are tall slender aquatic plants that usually grow in dense stands. Numerous staminate flowers occur above the pistillate flowers on a tall spike. Leaves are long and narrow with parallel veins. Common Cattail is an example of this family.

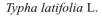

Virginia A. Phelps

Typha latifolia L.

Common Cattail

Staminate flowers are massed directly above the pistillate flowers. At maturity the latter turn brown. These perennial plants grow 3 to 8 feet tall in swamps, marshes, pond margins and ditches across Pennsylvania.

May-July

Phyllis T. Monk

Typha angustifolia L.

Narrow-leaved Cattail

This more slender Cattail has leaves less than 0.75 inch wide and there is a space on the stalk between the upper staminate flowers and the lower pistillate flowers. Narrow-leaved Cattail is less common than *T. latifolia* L., and grows in swamps, marshes, and ditches across Pennsylvania.

May-July

334

PONTEDERIACEAE
Pickerelweed Family

These plants have blue flowers on a spike. Leaves are broadly heart-shaped. They grow in shallow water or muddy shores. Pickerel-weed is an example of this family.

Pontederia cordata L.   Pickerel-weed

Growing in shallow, still water, Pickerel-weed has broad heart-shaped leaves up to 10 inches long and 6 inches wide. Blue flowers are borne on spikes 3 to 4 inches long on stalks that are 1 to 3 feet high. This plant grows in the upper northwest and eastern counties of Pennsylvania.

June-October

Esther G. Allen

335

LILIACEAE
Lily Family

These herbaceous plants are perennial, arise from bulbs, and have parallel-veined leaves. Flower parts are in threes. The term "tepal" is used for petals and sepals that are similar in form and color. This family includes lilies, tulips, trilliums and onions. Trilliums are representative of the family.

Trillium grandiflorum (Michx.) Salisb.   Large-flowered Trillium

The large, showy white flowers are 2 to 4 inches across and fade to a rosy pink. Leaves are 2.5 to 6 inches long in a sessile group of three on an 8 to 18-inch stem. The fruit is a red berry. This perennial herb arises from a stout rhizome. Picking this or other Trilliums will destroy the plant, and browsing deer have decimated many populations. Large-flowered Trillium is found in rich woods mostly in western Pennsylvania.

April-June

Esther G. Allen

Aletris farinosa L.

Colicroot

Tubular white flowers, each rough on the outside, have six flaring points. A stiff spike-like stalk, 1 to 3 feet tall, arises from a rosette of 2 to 6-inch lance-shaped, pale green leaves. It is listed in the Pennsylvania Wild Flower Conservation Act. This plant grows in dry, sandy soil, and is mostly a southern plant found rarely in Pennsylvania.

May-August

Esther G. Allen

Allium canadense L.

Wild Garlic
Meadow Garlic

The flower stalk grows 1 to 2 feet tall from an underground bulb. The slender stalk holds bulblets and a sparse flower cluster at the top. Before blooming, the cluster is covered with a two or three-parted papery bract that later falls off. The few erect flowers have six pink or white petals. Aromatic leaves are narrow, flattened and somewhat shorter than the flower stalk. This plant grows in moist meadows and open woods throughout most of Pennsylvania.

May-July

Robert F. Bahl

337

Robert F. Bahl

Allium cernuum Roth

Nodding Wild Onion

Similar to other onions, this plant grows from an underground bulb and has a 1 to 3-foot tall flower stalk. After the flowers open, the flower head droops. Six tepals are white or pink with protruding yellow stamens, each flower being about 0.3 to 0.8 inch long. The aromatic leaves are thin and are shorter than the flower stalk. The plant blooms on banks or hillsides in rocky soil in central and western counties of Pennsylvania.

July-August

Esther G. Allen

Allium tricoccum Ait.

Wild Leek
Ramps

The broadly tapering 8 to 10-inch leaves appear in April and by June wither away before the 6 to 18-inch flower stalk appears with a symmetrical tuft of whitish flowers. The plant arises from a bulb that has a sweet, spring onion flavor, and is the focus of southern Appalachian festivals in April. The plant may be found in rich woods in scattered locations throughout Pennsylvania.

June-July

Amianthium muscaetoxicum
  (Walt.) A. Gray

Fly Poison

    This plant sends up a flower stalk 2 to 4 feet tall with white to greenish flowers in a conical cluster. The flowers have broader tepals and are more closely spaced than the similar Bunchflower, *Melanthium virginicum* L. The basal leaves are grass-like but blunt-tipped, with a v-shaped midrib. They grow 15 to 20 inches long. Fly Poison is found in dry, sandy woods, and as "toxicum" suggests, the plant has poisonous properties. This plant is located primarily in central and eastern Pennsylvania.

Virginia A. Phelps

May-July

Camassia scilloides (Raf.) Cory

Wild Hyacinth
Eastern Camass

    The pale blue flowers have six tepals and six stamens. Along the flower stalks are several small narrow leaves. The leaves are 5 to 15 inches long, and the flower stalk is 1 to 2 feet tall. The basal leaves have a v-shaped midrib. The plant lives in moist meadows and along streams, and is found in a few counties of southwest Pennsylvania.

May-June

Virginia A. Phelps

339

Chamaelirium luteum (L.) A. Gray

Devil's Bit
Fairy Wand
Blazing Star

Devil's Bit has drooping 15-inch to 2-foot long stalks of tiny whitish flowers. The leaves are 2 to 8 inches long, narrow at the base and broadening to a blunt tip. The male plant (Illustrated), has numerous staminate flowers; the female plant (Not illustrated), has inconspicuous spikes of pistillate flowers, each of which is rounded and 2.5 inches long. These plants prefer moist soil in meadows and thickets throughout most of Pennsylvania.

Esther G. Allen

May-July

Clintonia borealis (Ait.) Raf.

Yellow Clintonia
Bluebead Lily

Named for the naturalist and New York governor, Dewitt Clinton, this member of the Lily Family has drooping 0.5 to 0.8-inch yellow flowers in clusters of two to eight on a single stalk. The flowers later mature into 0.2-inch blue berries that are borne upright. There are usually two to three shiny, oblong leaves per plant, and each leaf is from 6 to 12 inches long. Yellow Clintonia occurs in moist woods and open areas, and is found in mountainous regions of northern and western Pennsylvania.

May-July

Robert F. Bahl

Clintonia umbellulata (Michx.)
 Morong

White Clintonia
Speckled Wood Lily

The ball-like umbel of small white, green or purple speckled flowers on a single 8 to 16-inch high hairy stalk distinguishes this plant from its close relative, the Yellow Clintonia. It too is named in honor of DeWitt Clinton. The several ripened fruits are shiny and black. Usually five or six large leaves are nearly flat on the ground. White Clintonia usually grows at lower elevations in rich woodland soil, and is limited to the western half of Pennsylvania.

Virginia A. Phelps

May-July

Disporum lanuginosum (Michx.) Nicholson   Yellow Mandarin
Fairy Bells

The greenish-yellow bell-like flowers bloom at the tip of the stem and have two shiny, heavily veined leaves beneath. The flowers are 0.5 to 0.8-inch long. The alternating leaves on the stem are 2 to 4 inches long and covered with fine hairs. The flower matures into a reddish-orange ovate berry. The stem usually bends at each leaf junction. The plant grows 1.5 to 2 feet tall in mountainous regions in the rich woodlands of western Pennsylvania.

May-June

Robert F. Bahl

341

Erythronium albidum Nutt.   White Trout Lily

    White Trout Lily is similar in size, blooming time, habit of growth, and habitat, to the Yellow Trout Lily. It is distinct in having purple-tinged white tepals. The name reflects the trout-like speckles on the leaves. It is limited to the Susquehanna Valley and southwestern Pennsylvania.

April-June

Esther G. Allen

Virginia A. Phelps

Erythronium americanum Ker-Gawl.

Yellow Trout Lily
Adder's Tongue Lily

    Like most members of the Lily Family, Yellow Trout Lily has six tepals. The yellow flowers have a flush of purple on the outer surface and are 1 or 2 inches long, on 8 to 12-inch stalks. There are usually two leaves at the base of the plant, and these are about 3 to 8 inches long and speckled with purplish blotches. The plants spread from underground bulbs and form masses of plants that cover extensive areas in the flood plains of streams throughout Pennsylvania.

March-May

Hemerocallis fulva (L.) L.

Day Lily
Introduced

This common plant has 4 to 6 inch wide orange flowers. Often masses of narrow pointed leaves arise from spreading, perennial, underground stems. The leaves are about 0.5 inch wide and may be 2 feet long. The flower stalk is 3 to 6 feet tall, sturdy, and branched at the top. It has numerous buds and a blossom that opens for only one day. The petals are unspotted and face upward, distinguishing it from other orange-colored lilies. Many cultivated forms have colors ranging from deep red-purple to pale yellow. This plant is a garden favorite that has successfully escaped cultivation and now may be found along roadsides and in meadows in most of Pennsylvania.

June-August

John Kuehn

Hypoxis hirsuta (L.) Cov.

Yellow Stargrass

Yellow star-shaped flowers, 0.5 to 0.75-inch across, are six-pointed having six tepals. Hairy grass-like basal leaves are 4 to 12 inches long, and flower clusters, often in threes, top a hairy stem. This plant is found in meadows and open woods throughout Pennsylvania except northern counties.

April-September

Esther G. Allen

Lilium canadense L. ssp. *canadense*   Canada Lily
                                                          Wild Yellow Lily

    In Pennsylvania this lily varies in color from yellow to red. Two or more bell-like nodding flowers 2 to 3 inches across are purple-spotted inside and grow on a 2 to 5-foot tall stem. The plant grows from bulbs on an underground root-stock. This plant requires cool, moist habitats in woods, edges of bogs, and moist meadows. Although not endangered, Canada Lily is relatively uncommon in Pennsylvania and should be protected.

                                                          June-August

Emily Johnson

Virginia A. Phelps

Lilium philadelphicum L.

Philadelphia Lily
Wood Lily

This lily grows from 1 to 3 feet tall and the flower faces upward. The flower is red-orange, spotted inside, and there are spaces between the petals and sepals near the base of the 6 inch broad flower. The leaves are 1 to 4 inches long, ovoid, and in whorls along the stem. The plant grows from an underground bulb. This lily grows in dry woods and thickets, and is found mostly in the eastern two-thirds of the state.

June-July

Virginia A. Phelps

Lilium superbum L.

Turk's Cap Lily

Growing from 3 to 8 feet tall, this is the tallest of the red-orange lilies. Two to three flowers occur at the top of a stout stem. Purple-spotted tepals tightly recurved, form the "Turk's cap." A green star radiates from the inside of the center along each petal and sepal. Brown, velvety stamens project 2 to 3 inches below the drooping flower. Shiny leaves, 2 to 6 inches long, ascend the stem in whorls. Turk's Cap Lily grows in moist or marshy areas throughout most of Pennsylvania except in the extreme northeast.

Virginia A. Phelps

July-August

Maianthemum canadense Desf.

Canada Mayflower
Wild Lily-of-the-Valley

A dense raceme of tiny, four-petaled, white flowers covers the upper 1 to 2 inches of the flower stalk. The plant grows 3 to 6 inches high, each plant having two to three clasping, heart-shaped, shiny leaves. Covering the woodland floor, masses of these plants occur in patches that often extend over wide areas. After blooming, most of the flowers mature into speckled pale-red berries. Canada Mayflower is located throughout most of Pennsylvania in acid soil woods.

Phyllis T. Monk

May-July

Medeola virginiana L.   Indian Cucumber Root

This is a perennial plant with an unmistakable form. A mature plant will have a broad whorl of 6 to 12-inch wide shiny leaves at mid-stem and another whorl of four or five smaller leaves at the top of a 1 to 2.5-foot high stem. Several small flowers droop below the upper whorl of leaves. Each flower has six recurved yellow-green tepals and six projecting reddish stamens. The flowers mature into dark blue berries that are held erect from the top of the stem. This plant blooms in moist, rich woods throughout Pennsylvania.

May-June

Robert F. Bahl

Melanthium virginicum L.

Bunchflower

    The large terminal greenish-yellow panicles are usually polygamous. The lower flowers are perfect; the upper flowers are staminate. There are conspicuous double glands at the broad base of each petal. Linear leaves are 0.5 to 1.5 inches wide and are mostly basal. Bunchflower is a 3 to 5-foot tall perennial herb that arises from a rhizome on thick, rough stems. The upper parts of stems are pubescent. This plant grows in wet woods, thickets, low ground and meadows mostly in eastern Pennsylvania.

June-July

Virginia A. Phelps

Ornithogalum umbellatum L.

Star of Bethlehem
Nap-at-Noon
Introduced

    The flowers are 1 to 1.5 inches wide and have tepals that are white above with a waxy greenish stripe beneath. Clumps of grass-like leaves are 6 to 10 inches tall with a whitish midrib. This perennial plant grows from a bulb in fields, along roadsides, and in woods, primarily in the southern counties of Pennsylvania.

April-June

Robert F. Bahl

347

Polygonatum biflorum (Walt.) Ell. var. *biflorum*   Solomon's Seal

Greenish-yellow flowers are usually paired and pendulous arising from the leaf axils. Leaves are paired, lance-elliptic to ovate, and sessile. They are 2 to 4 inches long with a prominent midrib. The berries are blue-black and round. This plant grows 1 to 3 feet tall. It is a finely haired perennial herb that arises from a rhizome.

Downy Solomon's Seal, *Polygonatum pubescens* (Willd.) Pursh, (Not illustrated), is quite similar to this species except that its lower leaf is papery and drops off easily, leaving a scar. Both species are common in most of Pennsylvania.

A similar species, Great Solomon's Seal, *Polygonatum biflorum* (Walt.) Ell. var. *commutatum* (Schultes f.) Morong, (Not illustrated), has prominent veins the whole length of the leaves with three to five flowers at the leaf axils and grows from 2 to 8 feet tall.

May-July

Virginia A. Phelps

Smilacena racemosa (L.) Desf.

False Solomon's Seal
Solomon's Plume

A terminal panicle of tiny white flowers forms a 2 to 4-inch cluster at the end of the 1 to 3-foot tall arching stem. Ripening fruits are first red-speckled, then turn bright red in the fall. Alternate leaves are 3 to 6 inches long. This is a perennial herb that arises from a creeping rhizome, and is found in moist woods, on banks, and in thickets throughout Pennsylvania.

May-July

Virginia A. Phelps   Phyllis T. Monk

Scott J. Shriver

Smilacena stellata (L.) Desf.

Starry False Solomon's Seal

Creamy white flower clusters top the erect, zigzag stems. Leaves are 2 to 5 inches long, folded along the midrib, and pale bluish-green. The plant grows 8 to 20 inches tall from a forking, creeping rhizome. Black striped green berries are uniformly red in the fall. This plant is found in thickets, open meadows and moist banks, and is not common in Pennsylvania.

May-August

Virginia A. Phelps

Smilacena trifolia (L.) Desf.

Three-leaved False Solomon's Seal

A small spike of tiny white flowers tops the 4 to 8-inch high stem. In the fall the ripe berries are dark red. The two, three, or four sessile leaves are 0.5 to 1.5 inches long. This plant arises from a creeping rhizome and may be found in wet woods and bogs in a few northeastern and northwestern counties of Pennsylvania.

May-July

Stenanthium gramineum
(Ker-Gawl.) Morong

Featherbells

The whitish flowers, perfect or unisexual, are formed on a terminal panicle 1 to 2 feet long. This is a perennial herb with leafy, long stems. The leaves are usually folded and have the remains of old leaf bases, which are grass-like, 1 to 1.25 feet long and 0.2 to 0.9 inches wide. This plant is found in moist rich upland woods primarily in western Pennsylvania.

June-September

Hershel R. Leapman

Streptopus roseus Michx. var. *roseus*

Rose-twisted Stalk

Pink bell-like flowers droop from the axils of the upper leaves. Alternating along the 12 to 30-inch zigzag stem, the sessile leaves are 2 to 4.5 inches long. Plants arise from a rhizome, and fruits are bright red berries. This plant is found in cool, moist woods in a few south central and northwestern counties in Pennsylvania.

April-July

Esther G. Allen

Three whitish petals surround the large pink or white ovary. Three broad overlapping leaves often obscure the downward-flexed flower. The plant grows from 6 to 16 inches high, arises from a rhizome, and is found in eastern Pennsylvania, with a few sites in western Pennsylvania.

Drooping Trillium, *Trillium flexipes* Raf. (Not illustrated), has coarser leaves and the straighter petals are usually white, but may be pink or maroon. It is listed in the Pennsylvania Wild Plant Conservation Act and, is found in a few southeastern and western counties of Pennsylvania. Both species grow in moist rich woods.

May-July

Robert F. Bahl   Phyllis T. Monk

Trillium erectum L. var. *erectum*

Ill-scented Wake-robin
Red Trillium

Ill-scented flowers vary in color from deep red to creamy white. Three green sepals below the petals have parallel veins. Simple, erect stems 8 to 16 inches high bear a terminal whorl of net-veined leaves. This plant arises from a short stout rhizome. This Trillium is found in moist, rich woods throughout most of Pennsylvania except the south-east corner.

Jay B. Brown

April-June

Trillium nivale Riddell

Snow Trillium

Creamy white flowers and three bluish-green leaves top the 2 to 6-inch stem that may emerge through the snow. Stems are reddish and arise from a stout rhizome. This tiny Trillium is the earliest to bloom in the spring. This plant is listed in the Pennsylvania Wild Plant Conservation Act. It is often found on north-facing slopes, in the rich moist woods of south-western Pennsylvania.

March-May

Phyllis T. Monk

353

Trillium sessile L.

Sessile Trillium
Toadshade

The flowers are sessile, narrow, and either maroon or greenish-yellow. The three 1.5 to 6-inch leaves are mottled with pale green streaks. The plant grows from 4 to 12 inches tall in rich moist woods, mostly in western Pennsylvania.

April-June

Esther G. Allen

Esther G. Allen

Trillium undulatum Willd.

Painted Trillium

This dainty trillium is distinct in having uniquely wavey borders on the petals, and a chevron of crimson at the base of each petal. Flowers are 3 to 3.5 inches across. The three leaves are narrower than other Trilliums and are 3 to 8 inches long. This plant grows 8 to 15 inches high, and lives in damp, rich, acidic soils, in mountainous regions in woods or bogs throughout most of Pennsylvania.

April-June

Uvularia grandiflora J. E. Smith   Large-flowered Bellwort

This large-flowered plant has perfect, yellowish, nodding 1.5-inch flowers. The perfoliate leaves are 2 to 5 inches long. The plant grows 12 to 18 inches high. The stems of this species are usually stouter than those of the Perfoliate Bellwort, *Uvularia perfoliata* L. Large-flowered Bellwort is found primarily in rich woods in western and northern Pennsylvania, but is not very common.

April-June

Robert K. Grubbs

Uvularia perfoliata L.

Perfoliate Bellwort

The drooping, pale yellow, 1-inch flowers remain mostly closed. The stem appears to pierce the 2 to 5-inch long leaves. This plant grows 6 to 20 inches tall, and is quite common in rich woods throughout Pennsylvania.

May-June

Virginia A. Phelps

355

Uvularia sessilifolia L.

Wild Oats
Sessile-leaved Bellwort

Pendulous pale-yellow bell-shaped flowers hang down from the stem in the upper leaf nodes. Oblong leaves are pointed at both ends. Growing from a slender rhizome, this perennial plant reaches a height of 4 to 5.5 inches, and is found in moist or dry woods throughout Pennsylvania.

May-June

Virginia A. Phelps

Veratrum viride Ait.

False Hellebore
Indian Poke

Large clusters of greenish six-tepaled flowers grow at the top of a branched spike 8 to 20 inches high. The 6 to 12-inch long leaves are clasping, heavily veined and folded. Growing from a stout rhizome, the plant grows from 2 to 8 feet tall. This plant may be found in swamps, meadows and low ground throughout most of Pennsylvania.

May-July

Esther G. Allen

IRIDACEAE
Iris Family

These are herbaceous perennial plants that arise from rhizomes, tubers or corms. Leaves are flat, narrow and pointed. Flowers are covered with bracts and bloom singly. Flower parts are in threes. The Blue Flag is representative of this family.

Iris versicolor L.

Blue Flag
Northern Blue Flag

The 4-inch bright blue flower consists of three narrow upper petals and three stamens that flare above the deeply veined and yellow-tinged sepals below. Stems are stout, growing 2 to 3 feet tall from fleshy, horizontal, rootstocks. Stiff sword-shaped leaves are as tall as the stems, and sheath-like bracts cover the buds. It grows in marshes, wet meadows, roadside ditches and wet, rich woodlands throughout Pennsylvania.

Slender Blue Flag, *Iris prismatica* Pursh. (Not illustrated), is similar to this species, but is daintier, with grass-like leaves. This plant grows in similar habitats and is not common in Pennsylvania. It is listed in the Pennsylvania Wild Plant Conservation Act.

May-July

Phyllis T. Monk

Iris cristata Soland.   Dwarf Crested Iris

The flower consists of three narrow, bluish, upper petals, and three broader, bluish, down-curving sepals. Each sepal has a yellow and white crest in the throat. Perennial thickened rootstocks give rise to 1 to 3-inch stems with one or two flowers at the top. Several leaves clasp the short stem and are broadly pointed, from 4 to 6 inches long. Some leaves, not associated with stems, may be up to 9 inches long. This tiny iris is found in a few scattered counties in the southern and southwestern areas of the state near streams and hillsides. These plants are protected under the Pennsylvania Wild Plant Conservation Act.

April-May

Robert F. Bahl

Esther G. Allen

Iris pseudacorus L.

Yellow Iris
Introduced

Two to 3-foot tall stems, stiff sword-shaped leaves, equal to or higher than the stems, and bright yellow flowers distinguish this species. Three broad sepals below and three narrow petals above make up the 4-inch flowers. Several buds accompany the flowers. Introduced from Europe, Yellow Iris has become established in marshy areas and stream banks. This is the fleur-de-lis of France. It grows from fleshy underground stems, and is common in Pennsylvania.

May-July

Arethusa bulbosa L.   Dragon's Mouth Orchid

The 8 to 20-inch high stem rises from a bulbous corm, topped by a single magenta flower about 2.8 inches in height. The sepals and petals stand in a position best described as "pricked-up-ear effect." The dragon's downward-turning tongue has purple veins, a yellow crest and white fringes. A rare white form has also been found. The solitary narrow leaf does not develop until after the flower fades, so it is seldom noticed. Dragon's Mouth Orchid grows in open sphagnum bogs that are strongly acidic, and has been found mostly in the four corners of Pennsylvania.

May-July

Virginia A. Phelps   Robert F. Bahl

Aplectrum hyemale (Muhl. ex Willd.) Nutt.

Puttyroot
Adam-and-Eve

Puttyroot is so-named because its paired corms are filled with a mucilaginous material that was used by the colonists to mend broken pottery. Adam-and-Eve refers to the two corms. In the fall it produces a corrugated winter leaf, striped with silver, about 6 inches long. The leaf usually disintegrates by the time the flowers open. A low percentage of the plants present will bloom within any one year. The 16-inch stalk bears eight to sixteen flowers with yellow-brown sepals and petals and a wavy-edged, three-lobed white lip with crests. It is found sparingly in rich woods of southern Pennsylvania.

Virginia A. Phelps

May-June

Calopogon tuberosus L.   Grass-Pink

The Grass-Pink has one to three linear leaves low on the stem. About eight flower buds varying from light to deep pink top the stem and open sequentially. The lip is uppermost and bears numerous white bristles with yellow tips that mimic stamens. A heavy bee activates a hinge causing the lip to bend down, depositing the pollen on the bee's back. Grass-Pink grows in wet meadows and bogs, and is widely distributed in eastern Pennsylvania, with many sites in western Pennsylvania.

June-August

Robert F. Bahl

Corallorhiza maculata (Raf.) Raf.

Spotted Coralroot

Coralroot refers to the branched underground rhizomes. The Spotted Coralroot is the most widespread of this saprophytic genus, and also the most variable in color, ranging from brown, purplish, reddish to clear yellow. It is leafless with a terminal raceme of up to forty flowers. The sepals are the same color as the stem but the petals are lighter; the 0.4-inch lip is white and irregularly spotted with purple. The yellow form has an unspotted white lip. This plant, which goes dormant for years, grows in shady deciduous or coniferous forests, and is found throughout Pennsylvania.

Phyllis T. Monk

July-August

Corallorhiza odontorhiza
(Willd.) Nutt.

Autumn Coralroot

Autumn Coralroot, a leafless saprophyte, is small and inconspicuous. The slender stems are 4 to 8 inches tall with a loose raceme of five to fifteen flowers that rarely open completely. The drooping flowers are purplish or green with a white lip, scarcely 0.2-inch long. This plant grows in dark woods at scattered sites across southern Pennsylvania, as well as on Presque Isle.

August-October

Virginia A. Phelps

Cypripedium acaule Ait.

Pink Lady's Slipper

The single terminal flower, on an 8 to 20-inch stem has sepals and petals varying from yellow-green to maroon. The lip is an elongated pouch, 1.4 to 2.8 inches, with a deep longitudinal fissure. This pouch can be entered by large bees that must come out at the top, passing the pollen. Lip color varies from pale pink to maroon with darker veins. The paired, basal leaves are ribbed and pubescent, and grow up to 11 inches long. This plant requires very acid bogs or very acid dry woods, and is often under pines throughout Pennsylvania.

Albert Shriver

May-June

Cyrpripedium calceolus L
var. *parviflorum* (Salisb.) Fern.

Small Yellow Lady's Slipper

The sepals and much-twisted petals are a rich mahogany color. The lip is a clear yellow inflated sac, 0.8 to 1 inch across. Edges of the aperture are rolled inward. This slipper is only sparsely pubescent. This rare plant grows only in calcareous bogs and mossy swamps. There are a few sites in western Pennsylvania.

May-July

Virginia A. Phelps

Cypripedium calceolus L.   Large Yellow Lady's Slipper
   var. *pubescens* (Willd.) Correll

    The Large Yellow Lady's Slipper is variable in size, habitat, and character-
istics. This large slipper grows up to 28 inches tall, has six pleated leaves that
are 4.75 inches broad and has one or two flowers. Leaves and stems are densely
hairy. The upper sepal is wavy-edged, yellow with brownish striping. The lower
sepals are united behind the lip that is a dull to bright yellow inflated pouch. The
linear petals are 2 to 4 inches long, are the same color as the sepals, and are highly
twisted. Overall flower width is up to 5.8 inches. This plant is found in dry
woods and is of general but limited distribution in Pennsylvania.

April-June

Esther G. Allen

Epipactis helleborine (L.) Crantz

Helleborine
Introduced

    Leafy stems are 8 to 40 inches
tall, bearing up to fifty greenish-purple
flowers, 0.8-inch across in a raceme.
The small lip has a central constric-
tion with a maroon cup for nectar.
Helleborine, originally a European
species, has spread rapidly since first
discovered in 1879 in upstate New
York. Indifferent to soil conditions,
this plant thrives in partial shade
throughout Pennsylvania.

July-August

Virginia A. Phelps

367

Virginia A. Phelps

Galearis spectabilis (L.) Raf.

Showy Orchis

Showy Orchis is a low-growing plant 4 to 6 inches tall with oblong basal leaves 7.9 inches long. Three to ten flowers are in a loose raceme. The wavy-margined white lip hangs down, and the pink-purple sepals join to form a hood. This plant grows in open woods and ravines, often under hemlocks, and is generally distributed throughout Pennsylvania.

April-June

Virginia A. Phelps

Goodyera pubescens Willd.

Downy Rattlesnake Plantain

Up to eighty small flowers are carried in a dense spike on a 6 to 20-inch stalk. Curved petals and sepals form a helmet over the lip and column, appearing almost spherical. This orchid is densely pubescent on the stem and leaves. The basal rosette is readily visible with its blue-green blades about 1.6 to 3.5 inches long, with a network of white veins. This may be our most common orchid, and is found in dry woodlands throughout Pennsylvania.

July-August

Isotria medeoloides (Pursh) Raf.

Lesser Whorled Pogonia

This Whorled Pogonia is thought to be the rarest terrestrial orchid in the eastern United States. It differs from the Whorled Pogonia in several respects: the flower is cream-colored, the stem is whitish-green and hollow, the leaves are more pointed and expand fully before the bud opens; the length of the sepals barely exceeds that of the lip. This is an orchid of closely guarded locations, but two recent sites have been found in central Pennsylvania. This plant is listed in both the Federal Endangered Species Act and the Pennsylvania Wild Plant Conservation Act.

Virginia A. Phelps

May-June

Isotria verticillata (Muhl. ex Willd.) Raf.   Whorled Pogonia

The flower, rising above the leaf whorl on a short stalk, is striking for its maroon sepals that are 1.6 to 2.5 inches long, far longer than the 0.6-inch lip with its white tip and fleshy ridge. The bud opens before the leaves expand. Whorled Pogonia is easily overlooked because of its protective coloration. Five to six oblong leaves form a whorl on a 12 inch stem, which is purplish, smooth and hollow. Like many other orchids, the Whorled Pogonia tends to flourish for years, then disappears into dormancy for a period. Large colonies of this plant are often found in wooded areas in Pennsylvania.

May-June

Scott J. Shriver

Scott J. Shriver

Liparis liliifolia (L.) L.C.Rich. ex Lindl.

Lily-Leaved Twayblade

Both *Listera* and *Liparis* genera are known as Twayblades. Lily-Leaved Twayblade has two lustrous elliptical leaves that grow low on the stem. The angled stem, 12 inches tall, bears a raceme of five to forty flowers. The dull madder-purple flowers are translucent with a broadly rounded wedge-shaped lip, 0.4 to 0.5 inch long. Sepals and petals appear threadlike. This inconspicuous orchid grows in dry rich woods across the southern half of Pennsylvania.

May-July

Virginia A. Phelps

Liparis loeselii (L.) L.C.Rich

Bog Twayblade
Loesel's Twayblade

The Bog Twayblade is smaller than the Lily-Leaved Twayblade with five to twenty light-yellow flowers on an 8-inch stem. The yellow-green leaves are strongly keeled. The flowers are 0.2 inches across with thread-like sepals and petals and a 0.2 inch long lip. This plant inhabits bogs and deep woods, in scattered sites across Pennsylvania.

June-July

Listera australis Lindl.

Southern Twayblade

The five to twenty-five flowers are dark maroon with spreading sepals and a 0.4-inch long linear lip deeply cleft into two threadlike lobes. Two opposite ovate leaves midway up clasp the 8-inch purple stem. This plant grows in deep wet woods and shady bogs, and has been found in Chester and Warren counties.

May-June

Virginia A. Phelps

Listera cordata L.

Heart-leaved Twayblade

The Twayblades in this genus are among our tiniest orchids and are least visible due to mosquito-sized flowers. A slender stem up to 12 inches high bears a pair of opposite heart-shaped leaves about midway. Up to twenty-five 0.1-inch greenish or madder-purple flowers are loosely placed at the top. The 0.2-inch long lip is deeply divided into spreading, nearly linear lobes. This plant grows in mossy wet woods or edges of bogs in very few sites in Pennsylvania.

June-August

Robert K. Grubbs

371

Robert F. Bahl

Listera smallii Wieg.

Small's Kidney-leaf Twayblade
Appalachian Twayblade

A loose raceme of flowers is greenish or yellow-brown. The sepals and petals are very narrow. The lip is wedge-shaped, 0.3 inch wide and 0.4 inch long, and deeply notched with a tooth at the sinus of the spreading lobes. The pair of leaves is kidney-shaped. This plant grows only in deep dark forests, typically under rhododendrons. The range for this plant is restricted to the Appalachian Mountains.

June-July

Virginia A. Phelps

Malaxis monophyllos (L.) Swartz
var. *brachypoda* (A.Gray)
F.Morris

White Adder's-Mouth

As many as fifty greenish-white flowers, 0.15 to 0.2-inch broad, are closely attached to the stalk. The lip droops and is abruptly long-pointed. The 4 to 12-inch stem bears a single broadly pointed leaf, 2 to 4 inches long. The leaf clasps the stem part way up. This rare orchid grows in wooded swamps and is found in a few sites in the northern tier counties of Pennsylvania.

June-August

Malaxis unifolia Michx.

Green Adder's-mouth

A multitude of tiny green flowers is found on a 4 to 12-inch stalk. The raceme elongates as flowering continues. This slender plant has a single leaf clasping the stem midway. This easily overlooked plant is more common than the White Adder's Mouth, *Malaxis monophyllos* (L.) Swartz var. *brachypoda* (A. Gray) F. Morris, and is found in dry or moist woods, in open areas, across most of Pennsylvania except the far west counties.

June-August

Phyllis T. Monk

Platanthera blephariglottis (Willd.) Lindl.

White-Fringed Orchid

A dense raceme of twenty to thirty white flowers tops a leafy 24-inch tall stem. The 0.5-inch ovate lip is irregularly fringed. In Greek, the specific name means "tongue that is like an eyebrow," a very apt description. White-Fringed Orchid is found in very acid sphagnum bogs, in a few scattered stations across Pennsylvania.

June-September

Virginia A. Phelps

Robert F. Bahl

Platanthera ciliaris (L.) Lindl.

Yellow-Fringed Orchid

This orchid has three to four leaves sheathing the tall stem that bears a cluster of thirty to sixty yellow to orange flowers. The lip is 0.8-inch long and deeply fringed; the spur is 1.4 inches long. It is tolerant of wet or dry habitats that are sunny or shady. In Pennsylvania, it is found south of a diagonal line drawn from the southwest to the northeast corners.

July-August

Scott J. Shriver

Platanthera clavellata (Michx.) Luer

Club-Spur Orchid

Three to fifteen cream-colored flowers top the stalk and are rotated so the lip projects from the side. The oblong lip is 0.1 to 0.2-inch long with three obscure lobes at the tip; the spur is 0.4-inch and sometimes club-shaped. The Club-Spur Orchid has a slender stem up to 14 inches with one leaf midway on the stem. This plant grows in bogs and wet, mossy woods, and is generally distributed over Pennsylvania, but is more common in eastern Pennsylvania.

July-August

Platanthera dilatata (Pursh)
Lindl. ex Beck

White Bog Candles

White Bog Candles are densely many-flowered on a leafy stem up to 40 inches tall. The flowers have a 0.3 to 0.4-inch triangular lip, and a spur about equal to it. This is a plant of wet bogs, found only in far northwestern Pennsylvania.

May-September

Scott J. Shriver

Platanthera flava (L.) Lindl
var. *herbiola* (R.Br.) Luer.

Pale Green Orchid

The Pale Green Orchid is easily overlooked due to its color and small 0.4-inch flowers. The stalk may be 2 feet tall with several dark-green sheathing leaves. The ten to forty yellow-green flowers are in a compact spike with sepals and petals forming a hood. The lip is oblong with a triangular lobe on each side. The spur is 2.8 inches long. This plant grows in swampy woods and swales, and is generally distributed in eastern Pennsylvania.

July-September

Robert F. Bahl

375

Robert K. Grubbs

Platanthera psycodes (L.) Lindl.

Lesser Purple Fringed Orchid

The Lesser Purple Fringed Orchid has a leafy stem with thirty to fifty flowers in a dense raceme. The lip is 0.5 to 0.6-inch long and is cut into three wedges. The fringe on the lip is cut to less than one-third depth. The spur is 1 inch long. This flower blooms two to three weeks later than Greater Purple Fringed Orchid, *Platanthera grandiflora* (Bigel.) Lindl. The habitat may be woods or open fields but in permanently wet conditions, throughout Pennsylvania.

July-August

Robert F. Bahl

Platanthera grandiflora (Bigel.) Lindl.

Greater Purple Fringed Orchid

Thirty to sixty lavender-purple flowers top the 4 foot tall stem. The 0.4 to 1-inch lip of the flower consists of three wedges cut more than one-third deep. Overall this is a larger version of the Lesser Fringed Purple Orchid, *Platanthera psychodes* (L.) Lindl., and is very distinctive. Peak flowering occurs two to three weeks earlier than the Lesser Purple Fringed Orchid. This plant has general distribution across Pennsylvania in damp meadows, open woods and ditches.

June-July

Platanthera hookeri (Torr. ex A.Gray) Lindl.

Hooker's Orchid

    Hooker's Orchid has two nearly round basal leaves that are flat on the ground. They are 6 inches across, thick and glossy. The leafless stem is up to 16 inches high and bears a spike of ten to twenty-five green flowers. The tapering deltoid lip curves forward at the tip. The flower has a 1-inch spur. The lateral sepals are completely reflexed. It grows in dry, forested areas with a few sites in the Pennsylvania mountains.

May-August

Scott J. Shriver

Platanthera orbiculata (Pursh) Lindl. var. *orbiculata*

Large Round-Leaved Orchid
Pad-leaf Orchid

    Pad-leaf Orchid has some similarities with Hooker's Orchid (above) having two basal leaves 3 to 4 inches long that are fleshy and shining. This species, however, has one or two bracts on the stem and bears an average of ten white flowers. The linear lip is 0.6-inch, and there is a 0.8-inch spur which projects horizontally backwards behind the flower.
    Platanthera orbiculata (Pursh) Lindl. var. *macrophylla* (Goldie) Luer, Large Round-leaved Orchid, is a large variety of the above species. It has 8 inch leaves and a tall spike with more than twenty flowers. Both varieties grow in wet humus in deep shade, and are scattered throughout the mountains of Pennsylvania.

Robert F. Bahl

June-July

Platanthera lacera (Michx.) G. Don   Ragged Fringed Orchid

The Ragged Fringed Orchid is relatively inconspicuous due to its creamy-green color and threadlike fringed lip. The 0.6 to 0.8-inch lip is three-parted and deeply cut; the spur is 0.9-inch long. This plant is quite variable with eight to forty flowers on slender to stout leafy stems that grow 2.5 to 4 feet tall. It grows in either bogs or dry areas, and is widely but thinly scattered throughout Pennsylvania.

July-August

Esther G. Allen   Phyllis T. Monk

Platanthera peramoena (A.Gray) A.Gray

Purple Fringeless Orchid

This is similar to the Purple Fringed Orchid, *Platanthera grandiflora* (Bigel.) Lindl., but the lip is barely notched, not fringed. The loose raceme of thirty to fifty rose-purple flowers tops a leafy stem 25 inches tall. The 0.5 to 0.9-inch lip has three wedged divisions that are shallowly notched or entire. The spur exceeds the lip in length. This orchid has been found in the lower Susquehanna Valley and in southwestern Pennsylvania.

June-August

Robert F. Bahl

Pogonia ophioglossoides (L.) Ker-Gawl

Rose Pogonia
Snakemouth

The Rose Pogonia has a single flower, and midway on the 8 to 12 inch stem there is a single leaf. The pink lip is deeply fringed, veined with red, and crested with yellow bristles. "Pogon" is a Greek word for "beard." This orchid is found in open wet meadows and sphagnum bogs, and is spread thinly across Pennsylvania.

June-August

Scott J. Shriver

379

Robert F. Bahl

Spiranthes cernua (L.) L.C.Rich.

Nodding Ladies' Tresses

Up to sixty flowers are borne in a tight coil that appears to be several-ranked. The white sepals and petals form a tube with the creamy lip, which is wavy-edged and slightly notched.

Yellow Nodding Ladies' Tresses, *Spiranthes ochroleuca* (Rybd.) Rydb., (Not illustrated), is so similar that it is often mistaken for Nodding Ladies' Tresses. The plants are variable and may also hybridize.

Nodding Ladies' Tresses is usually found as colonies in marshy fields, wet meadows and ditches throughout Pennsylvania.

September-October

Jay B. Brown

Spiranthes lacera (Raf.) Raf
var. *gracilis* (Bigel.) Luer

Slender Ladies' Tresses

Slender Ladies' Tresses has a single spiral of up to forty flowers, but sometimes is so tightly twisted that it appears several-ranked. The basal rosette of leaves disintegrates before the flowers open. Individual flowers are white with a prominent green center on the lip, which is less than 0.4-inch across; sepals and petals join at the base to form a tube with the lip. This orchid is found in dry to moist woods and thickets in most of southern Pennsylvania.

July-October

Spiranthes lucida (H.H.Eat.) Ames

Shining Ladies' Tresses

Shining Ladies' Tresses has a showy basal rosette of leaves that are glossy. The tubular flowers are white with a bright yellow wavy lip. About twenty of these flowers are spiraled in three ranks. It is the earliest of the *Spiranthes* to bloom, and is found in wet meadows, ditches and bogs where there is a good supply of water. This orchid is thinly spread over Pennsylvania.

Robert F. Bahl

June-July

Spiranthes romanzoffiana Cham.

Hooded Ladies-tresses

Creamy white horizontal flowers are in three vertical rows along the stem. The upward-arching hood surrounds the shorter downward-curving lip. The bracts are longer than the flowers and continue down the stem past the flowers. Leaves are linear from near the base of the 4 to 16 inch stem. Found in bogs and meadows, this rare plant is found in northwestern Pennsylvania.

July-September

Phyllis T. Monk

381

Glossary of Botanical Structure

The following terms, explained below, are found in the plant descriptions in this Guide.

Achene - a small, dry, one-seeded fruit that does not split open.

Alternate – an arrangement of plant structures, such as leaves, that do not occur in pairs along the stem.

Annual – a plant that completes seed production in a single year or less.

Anther – the pollen producing part of the flower.

Apical – located at the growing tip of the upper part of the plant.

Aquatic – living in water.

Axil – the junction between a stem and a leaf.

Berry – a pulpy fruit that encloses seeds; examples, tomato, and grape.

Biennial – a plant that develops only non-reproductive parts the first year, and produces seeds the second year.

Bilateral – having two halves that are alike.

Blade – the body of a leaf.

Bloom – a thin, whitish, often waxy, covering.

Bract – a modified leaf arising from the stem and associated with a flower and/or leaf.

Bulb – a fleshy underground stem that has leaves modified for food-storage.

Calyx – a group of modified leaves beneath the petals of a flower taken collectively. They may be green or the same color as the petals (tepals). The leaves may be separate or joined into a tube.

Capsule – a dry, seed-bearing fruit that may or may not split apart at maturity.

Ciliate – having fringe-like hairs.

Cleistogamous – an inconspicuous, self-fertilizing flower.

Compound – a leaf composed of three or more leaflets sometimes on a rachis.

Corm – a fleshy stem modified to store food.

Corolla – the petals of a flower.

Corymb – a flat-topped arrangement of flowers at the end of the stem that has alternating flower stalks.

Cyme – an arrangement of flowers at the end of a stem with opposite-branching flower stalks.

Dioecious – having male and female flowers on separate plants of the same species.

Disk – in Asteraceae, the arrangement of tubular flowers in a receptacle.

Downy – covered with fine hairs.

Drupe – a fleshy fruit having a single stony pit; examples, cherry and peach.

Filament – the part of a stamen that supports the anther.

Fruit – a ripened, seed-bearing, ovary.

Glabrous – smooth, often shiny, without hairs.

Glands – a plant structure that secretes sweet, oily or waxy substances.

Glaucous – covered with a waxy powder, such as a blueberry.

Head – a dense cluster of stalkless flowers.

Herb – a plant whose stem dies back to the ground in winter.

Herbaceous – fleshy plants that lack woody, persistent stems.

Hybrid – a plant that results when closely-related species are crossed.

Incised – deeply cut into several lobes.

Indigenous – a plant that is native to the area where it is found.

Inflorescence – the flowering parts of a plant.

Involucre – the layers of bracts that cover the receptacle of a flower.

Irregular – a flower pattern that is not symmetrical.

Keel – the two lower united petals containing stamens and pistil in
the Pea Family.

Leaflet – a single blade of a compound leaf.

Legume – a plant that can convert atmospheric nitrogen into nitrates.

Lobe – the divided part of a leaf or other plant structure.

Midrib – the central vein in a leaf or petal.

Monoecious – a plant that bears both male and female flowers separately .

Naturalized – a plant that becomes established in an area, but
whose origin is elsewhere.

Nerve – an unbranched vein.

Node – the region of a stem where a leaf or flower stalk originates.

Oblong – a leaf or petal that is more than two or three times as long
as it is wide.

Ovary – the part of a pistil that produces ovules.

Ovule – a female structure that becomes a seed after fertilization.

Palmate – a compound leaf arrangement that has leaflets originating
from the same point.

Panicle – flowers arranged in irregular groups along the upper stem.

Parasitic –deriving nourishment from a living source.

Pedicel – a flower stalk.

Pendulous – drooping, or hanging downward.

Perennial – a plant that can grow from year to year.

Perfect – a flower that has both stamens and pistil(s).

Perfoliate – a leaf that surrounds its stem.

Petals – modified leaves, usually other than green, that surround
the pistil and stamens of a flower.

Petiole – a leaf stalk that connects the blade to the stem.

Pinnate – the opposite arrangement of leaflets in a compound leaf.

Pistil – a female plant organ divided into a terminal stigma, a style
and an ovary.

Pollen – a rounded, microscopic structure that contains the male gamete.

Pollinia – a fused sac of pollen, in Orchidaceae

Polygamous – a plant with mixed perfect and unisexual flowers.

Pome – a fleshy fruit that has a central axis with seeds; example, apple.

Prostrate – flat on the ground.

Pubescent – covered with short, soft hairs.

Raceme – flowers arranged alternately along a flower stalk.

Rachis – the central stem of a compound leaf.

Ray Flower – a flower with a strap-like petal; example, the white petal-like flowers of a daisy.

Receptacle – the expanded area at the top of the flower stalk that holds the flower parts.

Regular – having uniform shape or symmetry.

Rhizome – a fleshy underground stem.

Rib – the most prominent vein(s) of a leaf.

Rosette – a circular grouping of leaves, often at the ground.

Scape – a flower stalk that arises from the ground.

Scurfy – having dry, scaly particles.

Segment – a part of a divided leaf or petal.

Sepal – a modified leaf, usually green, below the petals of a flower. Sepals often cover the flower bud.

Sessile – arising directly from a stem, lacking a petiole.

Shrub – a woody plant that has more than one stem, and is smaller at maturity than a tree.

Spadix – a thickened stalk bearing tiny sessile flowers in the Arum Family.

Spathe – the single bract that encloses the spadix in the Arum Family.

Spur – a hollow projection in the petal of a flower.

Spike – an elongated flower stalk having sessile flowers.

Stamen – a pollen-producing organ consisting of a filament and an anther.

Standard – the upper flaring petal of a flower in the Pea Family.

Stigma – the terminal portion of a pistil to which pollen may adhere.

Stipule – a small leaf-like structure at the base of a leaf.

Style – the part of a pistil that connects the ovary and the stigma.

Succulent – fleshy or juicy plant tissue.

Tendril – a clasping, twining projection associated with vines.

Tepal – a sepal that is the same color and shape as a petal

Tuber – a fleshy rhizome used for food storage and vegetative reproduction.

Umbel – an umbrella-shaped flower arrangement.

Vascular – plant tissues that conduct food or water.

Veins – bundles of vascular tissues in plants.

Weed – an aggressive plant that grows where it is not wanted.

Whorl – a circular placement of plant structures such as leaves.

Wing – a flattened projection along a stem; or a lateral sepal in the Milkwort Family.

Glossary of Taxonomy

Usually descriptive terms from Latin or Greek are used in the names of plants. Knowing the meaning of these terms can help one understand more about the plant they describe. The following list of terms may be useful in learning more about the plants found in this Guide.

alba-, albi-, ...white
americana . . . . .of America
angustifolia . . . . .narrow-leaved
anthos . . . . .a flower
aptera . . . . .with wings
arborea . . . . .tree-like
arvense, arvensis . . . . . . .of planted fields
atropurpurea . . . . .dark purple
aurea . . . . .golden
auriculata . . . . .with ears
blattaria . . . . .moth-like
boreale . . . . .far northern
bulbosa . . . . .bulb-like
caerulea . . . . .sky blue
campestris . . . . .of the plains
canadensis . . . . .of Canada
canescens . . . . .hoary
caroliniana . . . . .of the Carolinas
coccinea . . . . .scarlet red
communis . . . . .common
cephale . . . . .a head
cristata . . . . .crested
divaricata . . . . .forked
elliptica . . . . .oval
floribunda . . . . .full of flowers
flora . . . . .flowered
foetida . . . . .ill-scented
glabra . . . . .smooth
groenlandicum . . . . .of Greenland
hastata . . . . .halberd-shaped
hirsuta . . . . .stiff-haired
humifusa . . . . .spreading on the ground
humilis . . . . .low
hypopithys . . . . .under a pine
laevis, laevigata . . . . . . .smooth
incarnata . . . . .flesh colored

japonica . . . . .of Japan
latifolia . . . . .broad-leaved
laxa . . . . .loose
linearis . . . . .long and narrow
lucida . . . . .lustrous, shining
lutea . . . . .yellow
macrocarpon . . . . .large-fruited
maculata, maculatum . . . .spotted
maianthemum . . . . .flowering in May
maritima . . . . .of the seashore
maximum . . . . .largest
moschata . . . . .musky
neglecta . . . . .overlooked
nigrum, nigra . . . . .black
nivale, nivalis . . . . .of the snow
officinalis, officinale . . . .of the marketplace
palustre, palustris . . . . . .of swamps or marshes
parvi . . . . .tiny
pilosa . . . . .hairy
procumbens . . . . .lying flat
punctata . . . . .dotted
racemosa . . . . .an elongated axis of stalked flowers
repens . . . . .running along the ground
reptans . . . . .low-branching
ringans . . . . .gaping open
rosea . . . . .rose-colored
sanguinea . . . . .blood red
sativa . . . . .sown, or cultivated
scorpioides . . . . .coiled
secunda . . . . .one-sided
septentrionalis . . . . .northern
sinistra . . . . .leftward
spectabilis . . . . .showy
spirea . . . . .a wreath
stamineum . . . . .with prominent stamens
stolonifera . . . . .having runners
straminea . . . . .straw-colored
stramonium . . . . .a swelling
stricta . . . . .upright
subulata . . . . .sharply pointed
sylvestris . . . . .of woodlands
tenax . . . . .tenacious
tenuifolia . . . . .slender leaved
tomentosa . . . . .furry
trifoliata . . . . .three leaved

umbellata, umbellulata . . .radiating from the center
uniflora . . . . .one-flowered
virginiana, virginica . . . . . .of Virginia
verna . . . . .of the spring season
versicolor . . . . .more than one color
virens, viridis . . . . .bright green
viscosum . . . . .sticky
vulgara, vulgaris . . . . . . .common, ordinary

Photographer's Credits

Esther G. Allen, Evelyn K. Anderson, Robert F. Bahl, Jay S. Brown, Mary Lou Brown, Werner E. Buker, Walter J. Gardill, Ted J. Grisez, Robert K. Grubbs, Mary Joy Haywood, Emily Johnson, John W. Kuehn, Hershel R. Leapman, Richard McDermot, Edith R. Mock, Phyllis T. Monk, Robert L. Morgan, Mary Judith Paoli, Virginia A. Phelps, Stanwyn G. Shetler, Albert Schriver, J. Scott Schriver, Laura Wirkkala

Bibliography

Britton & Brown. 1970. *An Illustrated Flora of the Northeast United States & Canada.* Volume 1, 2, and 3.
Dover Publication

Fenald, Merrit L. 1950. *Gray's Manual of Botany.*
American Book Company

Gleason, Henry R. & Arthur Conquist. 1991. *Manual of Vascular Plants of Northeast United States and Adjacent Canada.* 2nd ed.
New York Botanical Garden, Bronx, NY.

Kartesz, J.T. & R. Kartesz. 1980. *A Annotated Checklist of the Vascular Flora of the United States, Canada and Greenland.*
University of North Carolina Press, Chapel Hill, NC.

Leur, C. A. 1975. *The Native Orchids of the United States and Canada Excluding Florida.*

Newcomb, Lawrence. 1977. *Newcomb's Wildflower Guide.*
Little, Brown & Co.

Peterson, Roger Tory & Margaret McKenny. 1968. *A Field Guide to Wildflowers of Northeastern and Central North America.*
Houghton Mifflin.

Phillips, Nathan H. 1939. "A Brief History of the Botanical Society of Western Pennsylvania." *Trillia, Proceedings of the Botanical Society of Western Pennsylvania.* No. 10.

Rhoads, Ann F. and Wm Kline, Jr. 1992. *The Vascular Flora of Pennsylvania: Annotated Check List and Atlas.*
American Philosophical Society.

Wherry, Fogg & Wahl. 1979. *Atlas of the Flora of Pennsylvania.*
Morris Arboretum of the United States.

Index
Common Names

Index
Scientific Names